# Ellen Terry

D1605723

# *Pocket* BIOGRAPHIES

*Series Editor C.S. Nicholls*

Highly readable brief lives of those who have played a significant part in history, and whose contributions still influence contemporary culture.

*Pocket* **BIOGRAPHIES**

# *Ellen Terry*

## Moira Shearer

Sutton Publishing

First published in 1998 by
Sutton Publishing Limited · Phoenix Mill
Thrupp · Stroud · Gloucestershire · GL5 2BU

British Library Cataloguing in Publication Data
A catalogue record for this book is available from the British
Library.

ISBN 0-7509-1526-9

ALAN SUTTON™ and SUTTON™ are the trade marks of
Sutton Publishing Limited

Typeset in 13/18 pt Perpetua.
Typesetting and origination by
Sutton Publishing Limited.
Printed in Great Britain by
The Guernsey Press Company Limited
Guernsey, Channel Islands.

*For John,*
*with love and gratitude*

# CONTENTS

# CHRONOLOGY

| | |
|---|---|
| **1847** | **27 February.** Birth of Ellen Terry in Coventry |
| **1856** | Her debut as Mamillius in Shakespeare's *The Winter's Tale* |
| **1860** | Acts as Prince Arthur in Shakespeare's *King John*, Charles Kean's Company, Princess Theatre, London |
| **1862** | Plays at Bristol Theatre Royal; meets Edward Godwin; in London, meets George Frederick Watts |
| **1864** | **20 February.** Marries G.F. Watts |
| **1865** | Leaves Watts |
| **1867** | Plays Katherine to Henry Irving's Petruchio in a bowdlerised *Taming of the Shrew*, Alfred Wigan Company, Queen's Theatre, London |
| **1868** | Elopes with Edward Godwin |
| **1869** | **9 December.** Birth of Edith Craig |
| **1872** | **16 January.** Birth of Edward Gordon Craig |
| **1874** | **28 February.** Returns to theatre in *The Wandering Heir*, Charles Reade's Company, Queen's Theatre. |
| **1875** | Plays Portia in Shakespeare's *The Merchant of Venice*, Bancroft Company, Prince of Wales Theatre, London; Edward Godwin leaves her |
| **1878** | Plays title role in W.G. Wills' *Olivia*, John Hare Company, Court Theatre, London; marries Charles Wardell (stage name Kelly); joins Henry Irving at the Lyceum Theatre, London, as Ophelia to his Hamlet |

# *C h r o n o l o g y*

| | |
|---|---|
| **1880** | Plays her first Beatrice in *Much Ado about Nothing* at Leeds; Portia to Irving's first Shylock, Lyceum |
| **1881** | Plays Camma in Tennyson's *The Cup*; Desdemona in *Othello*, with Irving and Edwin Booth; separates from Charles Kelly (Wardell) |
| **1882** | Plays Juliet in *Romeo and Juliet* |
| **1883** | First of seven American/Canadian tours with the Lyceum Company |
| **1884** | Plays Viola in *Twelfth Night* |
| **1885** | Plays the title role in *Olivia*; Marguerite in Goethe's *Faust*; death of Charles Kelly |
| **1886** | Death of Edward Godwin |
| **1888** | Plays Lady Macbeth to Irving's Macbeth |
| **1892** | Plays Katherine of Aragon in *Henry VIII*; Cordelia in *King Lear*; George Bernard Shaw correspondence begins |
| **1895** | Henry Irving knighted |
| **1896** | Plays Imogen in *Cymbeline* |
| **1898** | Syndicate takes over Lyceum; equipment from forty-four Irving productions lost in fire at Southwark warehouse; Irving seriously ill; Ellen tours with Frank Cooper |
| **1900** | Buys Smallhythe Place |
| **1901** | Plays Volumnia in *Coriolanus*; Lyceum bankruptcy |
| **1902** | Plays Mistress Page in *The Merry Wives of Windsor*, Beerbohm Tree Company, His Majesty's Theatre, London |
| **1903** | Final *Merchant of Venice* with Irving at a charity matinée, Drury Lane Theatre, London; Ibsen's *The Vikings*, Imperial Theatre; in management with E.G. Craig |

# Chronology

1905    Death of Henry Irving; Ellen in J.M. Barrie's
        *Alice-Sit-By-The-Fire*

1906    Golden Jubilee at Drury Lane; plays Lady Cicely
        in G.B. Shaw's *Captain Brassbound's Conversion*

1907    Marries James Carew on American tour

1909    Carew leaves her

1910–21 Lecture tours of England, America and Australia

1925    Awarded DBE

1928    **21 July.** Death at Smallhythe

# INTRODUCTION

She was tall and fair. Her attractive face was mobile, her mouth wide, her voice musical. She had an abundance of nervous energy and her movements were quick and graceful. Her hands were unusually large, causing distressing self-consciousness in extreme youth. Later she would use them to great theatrical effect.

There are many claims for Ellen Terry as the greatest of all English actresses. Writers, during her lifetime and after, have tumbled over each other in praise, verging on idolatry. Yet they rarely mention her acting; the creation of character seems non-existent in their ecstasy over her appearance, personality, her entrances and exits and her all-pervading charm.

Her son, Edward Gordon Craig, has written that 'She played but one part – herself. And when not herself, she couldn't play it.'[1] Virginia Woolf wrote that 'Ellen Terry is remembered because she was

Ellen Terry.'[2] Max Beerbohm described a 'genial Britannia';[3] 'Our Lady of the Lyceum' was the amused phrase of Oscar Wilde, when this 'spiritual, divine'[4] woman attracted a near-religious awe.

As Henry James remarked, Ellen's was 'a face altogether in the taste of the period',[5] and perhaps this had much to do with her enthronement in the public heart, a public with an extensive female element. People went to the theatre to see their own lovable, unchanging Ellen and she played to them, drenching them with tears in emotional scenes. Her public wept with her.

This is not unlike the idolisation of the screen goddesses of the 1920s and '30s who, with few exceptions, gave 'personality performances' which thrilled their fans. No hint of the vulgar business of interpretation was allowed to spoil the glowing celluloid image, or fame and popularity might have vanished overnight. The faces were fashionable, indeed they set the fashion for millions of women round the world. Was this not Ellen Terry's secret too?

Her father, Ben, was saddened by her choice of 'security' and 'lovableness'[6] in the heyday of her career. He remembered her wild gift for comedy as a child and felt that she squandered her real talent in this easy wish to please. And Ben knew about acting; he fathered a dynasty of Terrys who made their mark upon the stage. Ellen is now the only one remembered, her position secure after a thirty-year partnership with Henry Irving in his celebrated Lyceum productions. But the whole family deserves recognition – they were a remarkable tribe.

 O N E

# BEN AND SARAH

Crown Street, Portsmouth, was the setting where young Ben Terry, son of a publican, and Sarah Ballard, daughter of a builder and master sawyer, played together as children. Ben had a touch of the Irish in his family, Sarah Scottish blood through her mother, a Miss Copley of 'superior' descent. Sarah was tall, graceful and fortunate in having a lovely, flexible voice which she would bequeath to her children; Ben was attractive, rather dapper and a bit of a tearaway, quite a lad with the girls.

In 1837, when the eighteen-year-old Victoria became queen, Ben, at twenty, was thrilled by the reopening of the little High Street theatre, sometimes known as the Portsmouth Theatre or the Theatre Royal. It had been closed the previous year 'for unseemly and improper conduct' but now, under the management of William Shalders, it took on a new, tidier life with better gaslighting, fewer icy draughts and a thorough airing from fires in the auditorium and backstage.

Ben, obsessed by all things theatrical, immediately wheedled himself into close contact with Mr, Mrs, and Miss Shalders, a staunchly professional trio who ran every aspect of the theatre themselves. This included acting, singing and dancing in support of visiting stars who passed by for occasional performances. Ben was there every night, leaning over the gallery rail, savouring every detail of Shalders's pirated versions of London dramas. He worked backstage in an invaluable apprenticeship, learning to repair, paint, scrub and glue together all types of prop and scenery, until a golden day when he was taken on as an extra drummer in the orchestra. This had been engineered by his brother, George, one of the violinists in the pit and the only Terry to understand and encourage Ben's unexpected passion.

William Shalders was an excellent craftsman in the theatre of his day. He gave Charles Dickens his first stage production of an early work and was later immortalised as the hilarious Vincent Crummles and Company in *Nicholas Nickleby*, with poor Miss Shalders presumably the model for the ghastly but glorious Infant Phenomenon. Did Ben, in later life, ever make the connection with his old mentor and family? Sadly, there is no record of it.

Sarah, meanwhile, listened with increasing pleasure and eagerness to his ideas and plans for the future. She had several suitors but was completely in love with Ben, a love that lasted to the day of her death. They read plays together and he described the life of a circuit company, sometimes dubbed strolling players; Sarah realised that such a life would be rough, poor and uncertain but she was fired by his enthusiasm and did not hesitate. Both were about to be twenty-one – they would marry without a word to their parents and leave with the current travelling troupe. And so it was. After a deal of subterfuge, Sarah left home with her friend, Eliza Mitchell, on the morning of 1 September 1838, to be joined by Ben and his cousin, Ned. Walking calmly as on any normal day, they arrived at St Mary's, Portsea, where the Reverend J.V. Stewart married them in full church ceremonial. Entirely happy, they bid goodbye to their secret witnesses and, without a single backward glance, set out on their lifetime adventure.

At the beginning it proved a harder life than Sarah had imagined. Travelling players of the nineteenth century were not unlike the 'Players' who erupt rumbustiously into Shakespeare's *Hamlet*, their conditions verminous and their public notoriety always that of 'rogues and vagabonds'. Neat, elegant Sarah, accustomed to white linen sheets and a gleaming dining table, blanched but coped wonderfully and was soon translated (for unspecified reasons) into Miss Yerret, a 'Walking Lady' in the troupe's productions.

Walking ladies and gentlemen were the lowest rung of the theatrical hierarchy; their tradition lasted into the 1920s. Plays were written to rigid specifications: Leading Man; Leading Juvenile; Heavy Man; First Old Man; First Low Comedian; Walking Gentleman. Then, Second Old Man and Utility; Second Low Comedian and Character; Second Walking Gentleman and Utility. For the women, First and Second Chambermaid were substituted for the Low Comedians.

Everyone knew his or her exact function and was employed accordingly. Only those in Utility faced uncertainty, sometimes acting a small role but often contributing animal noises or thunderclaps offstage, and probably changing scenery. Ben, with his exuberant ambition, found himself trapped in Utility, even when he and Sarah moved on to other troupes in the hope of better positions. These first hard years took their toll, Ben becoming a little less the jaunty young buck and poor Sarah quite worn.

In 1839 their first child, Benjamin, was born — luckily they were in lodgings at the time. Then came two girls, Kate named after Ben's mother and Ellen after Sarah's, but both babies died in infancy. While Sarah grieved, her resilient husband at last secured a good engagement at the Liverpool Theatre Royal. The play was Dickens' *Martin Chuzzlewit*, with real acting parts for them both; Sarah did her best to match Ben's rekindled ebullience but she was an exhausted twenty-seven-year-old and again pregnant. They had moved on to Falmouth when, in May 1844, the second little Kate Terry was born, a chubby, healthy baby whose father was already planning her golden stage future as she lay in her cot. Three years later in a Market Street tenement house in Coventry, a midwife would again hurry to Sarah's bedside, to deliver by candlelight a second little Ellen Terry. The date was 27 February 1847, the theatre within a few yards, as Ben rushed to and fro in anxious anticipation.

It was no lack of feeling that caused Ben and Sarah to give these babies their dead sisters' names; it was often the custom in Victorian families, suffering the pain of infant mortality so frequently. Strong, capable Sarah would give birth to six more children, all healthy and lively. George followed Ellen, then Marion (known as Polly), Florence (Floss), Charlie, Tom and Fred (Tops, the baby). Ben's cup would overflow when three daughters and Fred succeeded brilliantly in the theatre; their mother was to be less happy, longing for her girls to have real security and a more conventional pattern to their lives.

But, apart from Fred, it was her growing boys who gave Sarah her greatest worries. Solid, reliable George, with his gift for carpentry, would have a passable, if unspectacular career; handsome, charismatic Charlie would charm his way through anything that life might offer; but young Ben and Tom? What would the future bring to her weak eldest son and to Tom, the family black sheep?

It brought sadness to Sarah, watching the perpetual scrapes of good-hearted Ben, a compulsive gambler, and the darker escapades of incorrigible Tom – as sister Ellen put it, 'a fascinating wretch'.[1] They were shipped off to Australia and India, their desperate pleas for money regularly reaching home. Cool, elegant Marion seems to have been the most warmly maternal family member, subsidising her two difficult brothers for most of their lives.

Sarah did all she could, probably without their father's knowledge; in any case, he was always too wrapped up in the theatre, with his own unimpressive but useful acting and the burgeoning careers of his daughters. Sarah had another cross to bear as her cheerfully thoughtless husband 'strayed' with regularity. He was well aware of the attractive figure he cut and made the most of it.

Nevertheless, his devotion to Sarah was absolute. As the Terry family grew they continued to travel the country, living in any available lodgings and often acting in unlikely surroundings which brought in a pittance. The girls were taught by their parents to read, write and do sums, but that was the extent of their formal education, their theatrical training far outstripping everything else.

Poor Sarah — her one longing was for a little house of her own. She was, in many ways, a saint, forever toiling for her brood who loved and admired her, but in the undemonstrative, rather careless way of children. Ellen, so much her father's daughter from her first breath, would realise in later years just how great Sarah's sacrifice had been.

*T W O*

# KATE AND ELLEN

Little Kate was the first Terry child star. On the stage from the age of three she was coached, even drilled, by her eager father; elocution and the projection of the voice was his forte, allied to song and dance which was compulsory in the productions of the nineteenth century. Her career began with nymphs and fairies, through which she flitted gracefully, graduating to a solo number entitled 'I'm ninety-five', performed in bonnet and shawl, which not unnaturally stopped the show.

Toddler Ellen – Nelly to everyone – watched all this with a mixture of interest and boredom, impatient for her own chance in the limelight and her father's sole attention. The little girls were poles apart in temperament, Kate docile and exact, Nelly noisy and impatient. As they grew older their appearance mirrored their characters, Kate short, neat and dainty, Nelly large-limbed and gawky. As Kate's career prospered Ben turned his sights on

Nelly, so like him and undoubtedly his favourite child. She went through the same rigorous vocal regime as her sister, understanding and enjoying it, and her excellent articulation through 'a slightly veiled voice'[1] would always be a tribute to this early training.

Meanwhile, the travelling continued and, in Edinburgh for a production of Shakespeare's *King John*, Kate had her first real critical acclaim as the boy Prince Arthur. It was rather too much at her tender age and it went to her head – 'poor little conceited Kate',[2] sighed her mother with absolute understanding.

But her Edinburgh success was to bring an important enrichment to the Terrys. They had moved on to Liverpool in 1851 when Ben received a letter from Charles Kean, son of the celebrated 'lightning flash' Edmund Kean, requesting Kate's attendance for audition at the Princess Theatre in London's Oxford Street. Ben and Sarah were thrilled, but for different reasons – he, solely for the advancement of his talented child, and she, loving Kate, but also yearning for a morsel of financial security to aid the education of less theatrical young Ben.

The unpretentious Princess had quite a noble history, having been home to the Vestris management, followed by that of the famed actor-manager William Charles Macready. On his retirement in 1850, the well-educated, dry-as-dust Charles Kean took over. Kean was a pedestrian actor but had a remarkable wife in the former Ellen Tree, a lovely actress (whom Kean had pinched from an early Macready company) who had become a formidable *grande dame* of the stage and an exceptional teacher of young actors.

In her forties, Mrs Kean had lost her looks but not her talent which far outshone that of her husband. She still played her Beatrices and Lady Macbeths but in a strange guise – full crinoline and coiffure à la Queen Victoria. She was never seen otherwise, even in daily life. Yet she was never a figure of fun; the young loved and respected her, sensing the theatrical knowledge and expertise she gave them in rehearsal. Nelly, when her turn came, would realise the deep debt she owed to this eccentric woman.

In Liverpool, Sarah – full of misgivings, knowing Ben's 'frailty' – set off for London with Kate in her 'best', young Ben and baby George. Five-year-old Nelly stayed with Ben in the north while he completed an engagement. Luckily, after Kate's successful audition and initial performance, Kean offered Ben employment in his company and the family was united on the top floor of a house in Gower Street. Sarah, no longer 'Miss Yerret, Walking Lady', decided to join the Princess's wardrobe department – she was, after all, an expert seamstress, making all her children's clothes. With a touch of snobbery, Ben felt angry and humiliated, but she had no false pride, knowing that the little extra was needed for young Ben's schooling.

In the next few years this amazing woman produced Polly, then Charlie, then Floss, her pretty and most universally loved child. They were all born in the Gower Street flat, while Kate achieved increasing success with the Keans. Nelly came to the theatre too, watching everything – particularly Mrs Kean – and attending Oscar Bryn's dancing class in which she shone. Later in life she would say that she learnt to walk well in his admirable lessons.

The 1855/6 season included a production of *The Winter's Tale*, with both Ben and Kate cast in small roles. From a posse of child actors, Mrs Kean chose Nelly to play Mamillius with his little go-cart, her début in a London theatre. On 28 April 1856 proud Ben appeared with his two daughters before an audience which included the Queen, the Prince Consort, and an unknown young tutor from Christ Church, Oxford, who would remember the Terry family when he became world famous as Lewis Carroll.

The excitement of playing Mamillius in front of a big, live public was soon forgotten when Nelly was given the role of Puck in the Keans' truncated version of *A Midsummer Night's Dream*. The cutting and, indeed, mutilation of Shakespeare's plays was still the common practice in the nineteenth century. Nevertheless, the role of Puck remained a considerable challenge to young Nelly; she faced it with aplomb, enjoying herself and capering engagingly. One performance was watched by a budding young architect from Bristol, Edward Godwin, who might have been greatly startled had he known that, thirteen years later, Puck would be the mother of his children.

Kate, understudying and playing Titania, was still the diminutive family star, yet it was she, not Ben, who realised the necessity for change from the now cramped top floor conditions at Gower Street, with its flights of stairs. She achieved it and they moved to a terraced house at 92 Stanhope Street, Kentish Town, an area which was still countrified in the 1850s. There was a little more money from raised salaries, a great deal of bargaining at furniture sales and much delight that the family at last had a home of their own. The small paved yard with an ivy-clad wall at the back became their garden – they were blissful. Soon after they were settled, the Princess Theatre closed for its four-month summer break and all actors had to find other employment. Ben, not for the first time, rented a tiny theatre at Ryde, across the Solent from their old homes in Portsmouth. The family lived in a cottage near the beach and, while the younger children enjoyed a seaside holiday, Ben put on two-handed farces starring Miss Kate and Miss Ellen Terry. Kate played demure young girls and looked enchanting, Nelly, in comic ballooning trousers, played naughty younger brothers or visiting popinjays who smoked cigars. She was eight years old and had enormous success with a theatrically naïve public, but this was the moment when Ben realised that her gift for comedy was exceptional.

Nelly, herself, loved playing boys and behaving badly on stage. She enjoyed making an audience laugh and hearing its vigorous applause at the final curtain. She became more and more uninhibited in her performances and in her off-stage behaviour; Kate may have suffered from some early conceit but it was as nothing compared to the way Nelly now threw her weight about. She was a profound embarrassment to her sister.

This continued on their return for the new season at the Princess, Nelly imagining herself a great star. The company men were much amused, treating her as a joke, but to the women she was an absolute pain. Mrs Kean viewed her with a steely eye. Quiet, politic Kate was steadily advancing to leading roles; she played Ariel in *The Tempest* and, as Cordelia in Kean's *King Lear*, she became an overnight star. But the over-elaborate production of *Lear* lost money and, with the Keans' theatre lease running out, they decided on a farewell season in 1860.

It began with an indifferent *Merchant of Venice* which was quickly replaced by *King John*, Nelly now cast as Prince Arthur. Mrs Kean was ready. Through rehearsals continuing into the night, this acute woman knocked the nonsense out of Nelly, gave her invaluable guidance on real acting and brought about a performance of genuine depth. It also brought critical success which the child was sensible enough to appreciate, though it did not prevent her careless Fleance in the following production of *Macbeth*. She still had a lot to learn.

As the Keans' reign ended, the Terry girls had, in fact, learned more than they realised at the time. Apart from Mrs Kean's inestimable contribution, they had been exposed to productions of astonishing accuracy; Charles Kean may have been a wooden actor but his knowledge of history, architecture, scenic design and costume gave a rare beauty and authenticity to his plays and attracted a discerning public. Unconsciously, the young members of his company acquired new standards of taste and discrimination which coloured their future careers. This was Kean's legacy and it proved, for Nelly in particular, a foretaste of the exquisite settings she would enjoy in her Lyceum years.

The girls' development was further enriched by their introduction into an artistic group of painters and writers, which occasionally included interested members of London society. Two gifted young men were responsible for this added education, both barristers, both fellows of their Oxford and Cambridge colleges, and both playwrights and critics. Charles Reade and Tom Taylor were much taken with Kate in her charming performances and invited her, with Nelly too, into their circle.

The girls listened to riveting conversation, met fascinating people and visited grand London houses, though Nelly in her *Memoirs* would recall her greatest pleasure in Sundays spent at Tom Taylor's beautiful house and garden in Lavender Sweep. These two influential men became her lifelong friends, Kate having left the stage at the height of her career for a rich and happy marriage. Charles Reade would one day play a crucial part in Nelly's future.

## THREE

# FOLLY

With the fall of the curtain on the final Kean season, the Terry family's plans went into action. Ben's mother had recently died, leaving him several hundred pounds and, with this legacy, he took the lease of the little Royal Colosseum in Regent's Park. It was an exhibition hall with a concert room boasting a tiny stage on which the Misses Kate and Ellen would appear in what he was pleased to announce as 'A Drawing-room Entertainment'. It was a clever move – the informality was particularly attractive to the scores of visitors strolling through the park. A young pianist, Sydney Naylor, was recruited and the girls acted several roles in two plays, reminiscent of the farces at Ryde.

They were an enormous success, Nelly scoring heavily as the cigar-smoking schoolboy. Ben made a profit before the end of the Colosseum lease and they then toured the West Country with similar success. Although their circumstances were much

improved the travelling was not unlike that of Ben
and Sarah's early days with the circuit companies.
There was sometimes a carriage but often many
miles were travelled on foot; the girls and young Mr
Naylor enjoyed every minute of the lovely country
in fine weather, but the journeys exhausted Sarah,
who was again pregnant.

The family was reunited in Stanhope Street in
time for Kate's new engagement at the St James's
Theatre. Nelly, who was at a loose end, registered
her name with a theatrical agent. The St James's was
under the management of Mr and Mrs Alfred
Wigan, another pair of redoubtable theatricals,
Leonora Wigan being much in the mould of Mrs
Kean. Their leading lady (who would soon take over
the management) was the beautiful Miss Herbert,
whom Kate understudied while playing only small
and walk-on parts, which displeased her father.

Almost at once, Nelly was summoned for an
audition with the exotically named Mme Albina de
Rhona, a French actress and dancer whose
successful European career had brought her to
London and further success. She had taken the lease
of the Royal Soho Theatre, which she immediately
renamed the Royalty. Here she presented a series of

fairly dreadful, but popular, melodramas. The audition went well – Mme de Rhona liked the look of the lanky but attractive fourteen-year-old and engaged her on the spot. In the next few months Nelly would have the time of her life in these awful plays, behaving badly on the stage yet again.

But Kate's moment had come. Miss Herbert was taken ill and, at short notice, Kate played the Lady Ormonde in an adaptation of Sardou's *Nos Intimes* and created a sensation. The critics vied with each other in rapturous praise of her performance – it was clear that Kate Terry had 'arrived'. Even so, while the family celebrated quietly at Stanhope Street, Ben assessed her future; he was well aware that the return of Miss Herbert, after Kate's too-great triumph, did not suggest future harmony. She would be denied any further progress in the company. He also knew that she would now be welcome at any of the great theatres – Drury Lane, the Lyceum, the Haymarket – but felt that she still had much to learn.

Kate was as level-headed as her father. She agreed instantly to accept the offer from J.H. Chute of the Bristol Theatre Royal, where his Stock Company would give her experience in the widest variety of roles. The family divided again, Ben going with Kate to Bristol while Sarah remained at home, trying to keep Nelly under control. Nelly was learning nothing with Mme de Rhona, simply racketing about in the melodramas, so it was to Sarah's intense relief that, late in 1861, she could take Nelly to Bristol to join her father – and then the company, with sister Kate.

The year 1862 was happy and profitable for the girls. Chute had gathered a strong company in the beautiful Theatre Royal, actors who included Marie Wilton, later to marry Squire Bancroft, and Madge Robertson, later Mrs Kendal, who was always a rival to Nelly. Kate played Portia and Beatrice, with Nelly as Nerissa and Hero, and the public were beguiled, especially young men who haunted the stage door night and day.

Among many invitations, the Terry girls accepted one to a 'Reading Party' from the young architect, Edward Godwin, who lived with his wife in Portland Square. Architect friends of the Godwins took part in the entertainment and read *A Midsummer Night's Dream*, which Chute would soon produce. The girls were greatly admired, while they had eyes only for the unusual décor of Godwin's house: a few Persian rugs on polished floors, the minimum of furniture and Japanese prints covering plain pale walls. It was the starkest possible contrast to the heavily ornate rooms of Victorian taste and it made a tremendous impression on Nelly; she loved the airy space and the simplicity, the light shining through windows unimpeded by thick curtains. Kate's reaction was completely different and provided a perfect example of the temperamental gulf between them. On returning to their lodgings in Queen Square, she said quietly to her mother, 'I don't think Mr and Mrs Godwin can be very well off; they've got no carpets and hardly any furniture!'[1]

The Godwins continued their kindness and the girls visited their house many times, despite the wariness of Sarah who, perhaps, had one of those premonitions which often strike women. Godwin's taste in dress and theatre costume was another attraction for Nelly and, when she came to play Titania for Chute, Godwin designed her unusual dress. He bought the silk, cut it out, soaked it in water, then showed her how to tie-and-dry it in the eastern way. She was amazed, but the finished crinkled, clinging article was lovely and exactly right for the part. It gave her an attitude to theatre costume which she would never lose.

The golden Bristol season came to an end. Kate had perfected her trade, not only on the stage but in dealings with colleagues and with the adulation of lovelorn young men. Returning to Stanhope Street, in the nick of time for rascal brother Tom's birth, Kate was now ready for her rightful place – leading lady at the Lyceum. She partnered the English-German-French Charles Albert Fechter, a star of the day; to the family's delight she played many roles triumphantly and was much admired by Charles Dickens.

Nelly had *not* fully benefited from Bristol and was still, at fifteen, too much her father's spoilt favourite. Engaged to play at the Haymarket, she fell out with the manager, then with the leading actor, and finally with the company. Nothing was right; she disdained the coarse scandal-mongering of theatre gossip and was irritated by what she now regarded as the 'tawdry' world of the stage. Reade, Taylor, Godwin and their friends had shown her a different world, one she preferred and longed to join. Unfortunately, she would shortly do so and in ironic circumstances – through the admiration of an ageing painter for her brilliant sister Kate.

George Frederick Watts, the fashionable portraitist of society and the famous, had been smitten by Kate's stage appearance and wished to paint her. He was a singularly unattractive man of forty-six, with wispy hair and long straggling beard, but his professional success had secured for him a rich and doting patron. He lived in the studio annexe of Little Holland House, the guest of Mrs Thoby Prinsep, one of those society women who fancy themselves uniquely 'artistic' and enjoy the cachet of their own tame celebrity artist – in this case in permanent residence.

Watts was in clover, waited upon, cosseted, and given the ridiculous title 'Signor'. Mrs Prinsep's younger sister, Julia Margaret Cameron, came to his studio to take many of the photographs of eminent sitters which would make her famous, and the regular Prinsep 'salon' attracted the cream of the *beau monde*. The fact that Watts was supremely vain and self-centred and without a scrap of feeling for anyone seems to have passed unnoticed.

Tom Taylor was responsible for Kate's introduction into this hothouse. She could not attend the artist's studio without a chaperone, and, as Sarah was caught up with the younger Terrys, it was Nelly who willingly accompanied her. They walked from Hyde Park through lovely open country and found Little Holland House near a farm. To Nelly it seemed idyllic.

Watts began his portrait of Kate. As it progressed he became more and more conscious of the younger sister and her romantic looks, and, before long, Nelly was included in the painting which he entitled *The Sisters*. Watts was enchanted; he already knew that Nelly would be the perfect model for future pictures he was planning. And she was flattered by this admiring attention, though her main pleasure lay in her surroundings – the elegant house and lovely gardens.

Behind the scenes a mild conspiracy was taking place, one which had been simmering for some time before the Terry girls' arrival. Mrs Prinsep was worried; Watts had shown more interest than usual in one or two attractive sitters – would he perhaps marry and leave her prestigious patronage? It was unthinkable . . . but, perhaps, if Watts married someone young and malleable who would move into Little Holland House and be easily dominated . . . ? Mrs Prinsep consulted Tom Taylor who, knowing Watts' admiration, suggested Kate Terry as the ideal young woman. Taylor seems genuinely to have believed that Kate would happily leave the theatre and stardom to be the wife of a middle-aged painter.

On meeting Kate, the older woman had to think again. The famous young actress turned out to be self-confident, decisive and in control of all situations; she simply would not do. But there was the younger sister, naïve and lacking self-assurance – and Watts was obviously greatly taken with her. Could *she* provide the peace of mind that Mrs Prinsep sought?

So this selfish woman set to work, aided by Tom Taylor. When Nelly came to the studio Mrs Prinsep was charm itself, welcoming the young girl as if she was one of the family and showing disarming kindness – an insincerity which Kate would have seen through instantly but in which Nelly basked and believed. Taylor, meanwhile, painted a rosy picture to Ben and Sarah of the wonderful opportunity for their daughter as the wife of a successful artist, immortalised by beautiful portraits. He must have known that he was playing on Sarah's longing for security and social 'betterment', and on Ben's present dismay at his favourite child's development.

Nelly's disenchantment with the theatre was a bitter blow and Ben would never understand it. He knew she was in thrall to people and a way of life that were neither suitable nor right, but found himself powerless against the Prinsep–Taylor onslaught. And powerless, too, against Nelly's disinterested failure at the Haymarket. Though there were differences of emphasis, the paramount misgiving of both parents must have been the unprepossessing Watts, now a forty-seven-year-old suitor for their teenage daughter.

The great friends, Reade and Taylor, fell out badly over this ghastly match but Prinsep power won. There was no proposal from Watts; Nelly, at home in Stanhope Street, received news of his 'request', was overwhelmed and accepted, and the die was cast.

What on earth made her say yes? It is incomprehensible, after her theatre childhood and her much-loved father's faith in her talent. Did she long for more education? Was she discouraged by her sister's success and fame? Or was it simply her youth and the rebellion of an adolescent? It surely cannot have been the physical attraction of Watts. Whatever the truth there was no going back. The wedding took place on the bleak morning of 20 February 1864, a week before Nelly's seventeenth birthday. She wore a brown silk dress designed by Holman Hunt and her only support was her father; no other Terry came to St Barnabas Church in Kensington for the doom-laden event. Reade's absence was predictable but where was Taylor? It seems extraordinary that this main player in the mini-drama was also absent and no adequate reason has ever been recorded.

Poor Nelly, it was all too much for her and, as the service ended, she burst into tears. As they walked from the church Watts made the single comment, 'Don't cry – it makes your nose swell.'[2] There was no honeymoon, no 'going away'; a carriage took them back to Little Holland House, with Mrs Prinsep in full command. Nelly would shed many more tears in the days ahead before her natural high spirits came once more to the surface, though they did so against much opposition.

Her idealised perception of life in the beautiful country house took a sharp knock when she became the unimportant Mrs Watts. Her one function was to pose for her husband's work and this she enjoyed, feeling that she was part of a great artistic accomplishment. She was still slightly in awe of Watts, despite the cold, thoughtless treatment he meted out. But any ideas she may have had of presiding over his dining table, entertaining his Pre-Raphaelite friends, were quickly shattered. She was foolish even to have thought this possible.

Mrs Prinsep's salons and grand dinner parties were rife with intrigue and with the decadent preciosity described by George du Maurier. Nelly was at first allowed to be present, where she saw her husband, in velvet, reclining à la Recamier on a sofa, with languid hand acknowledging the tributes of his peers. This brought out the hoyden in her; she began to behave badly, letting down her hair, wearing a short Greek tunic and kicking her legs around, and once, it was rumoured, appearing with no clothes on at all. After these misdemeanours she was banned from all social occasions.

Watts, without a glimmer of loyalty or under-standing, became chillier still as Nelly grew thin and spiritless. Her one pleasure at this time was a weekly visit to shabby Stanhope Street, to the welcome of her parents and brothers and sisters, who gave her renewed strength to return to her ill-chosen life. But she never complained, never gave her family any hint of her unhappiness – she simply hoped for better times.

*FOUR*

# GODWIN

The attractive architect Edward Godwin came from the West Country to London in October 1864. His young wife had recently died and, though continuing his Bristol practice with his partner, Crisp, he moved to no. 23 Baker Street to start design work in the capital. He knew Watts slightly, came to Little Holland House to Nelly's delight, and was soon a regular visitor. She found him an engaging companion and, luckily, Watts liked him too, enough for him to accompany his wife on reciprocal visits to Baker Street.

The whole aspect of Nelly's life changed with the arrival of Godwin. She listened and talked with him for hours about the theatre, Shakespeare, design and dress, all the things she had abandoned and now realised that she missed. Her spirits returned, and she was really happy in his company, while he was gradually falling in love with her. Watts, wrapped up in himself, was quite content for Nelly to call at

Baker Street alone; he knew, if he ever thought about it, that others were always there, busy with architectural work. Nelly's feelings for Godwin at this time have never been recorded.

Perhaps Watts' 'content' with her friendship had much to do with his own feelings of the moment. He had expected to mould Nelly to his way of life, to educate 'the child' as he called her; it had been hopeless and her erratic behaviour irritated him beyond words. He also now realised that he had reached the limit in portraying his wife in paint – she was no longer a source of inspiration. Mrs Prinsep watched with increasing pleasure. She had given Watts the chance of marriage; it had been disastrous and he would not wish to risk it again. Now, all that remained was to be rid of Nelly.

As a woman of craft and calculation she could have achieved this with ease, but there was no need – Nelly achieved it for her. The story has been told many times; how Nelly went one evening to Baker Street to find Godwin ill with a high fever, how she felt unable to leave him alone without help and stayed all night, sleeping in a chair and rising from time to time to apply cold compresses. In the morning he was better and, very tired, she took a cab back to Little Holland House. It is a plausible enough story, and could have happened like this; but why, if Godwin was so ill, did she not send a message to Watts or, better still, to Stanhope Street, for a member of the family to come to stay with her and provide further help?

Whatever the truth of that night, she was utterly compromised. On her return she found not only the Prinseps but her parents, who had been summoned for a full inquisition. She gave her story but was, of course, disbelieved and Ben and Sarah left in a numbed and wretched frame of mind. Watts, unsurprisingly, was nowhere to be seen while Nelly was being banished forever from Little Holland House society, and later – while she still lived in the annexe in a kind of purdah – he announced that he would never speak to her again.

Godwin's behaviour, throughout this drama, is inexplicable. He was the one person who could have supported Nelly, confirmed his illness and her care of him on that night, and he was silent. Not only silent but invisible, as he disappears completely from all accounts of the next weeks and months. Was this Victorian hypocrisy or the most eloquent comment on the whole affair?

Miserable and estranged from Watts, it was Nelly who finally begged to be allowed to return home, thus bringing her marriage to an end. Later, the triumphant Mrs Prinsep would arrange the legal dissolution, leading the ineffectual Watts by the nose as usual. Back in her own room in Stanhope Street, looking out over the brick-walled yard, Nelly was forced to confront her conduct and it did not improve her temper. She flared up continually with all the family, once shutting terrified, screaming young Fred in a cupboard – in late middle age he could still say, 'I hated Nell ever after.'[1] Bored and unhappy, her anger made a bad time worse. Was she still in touch with Godwin? Did she ever visit Baker Street? A Victorian veil again descends over this aspect of her private life – no one knows.

While Nelly languished in Stanhope Street, unsure of herself and her future, Kate had transferred to the Olympic Theatre as leading lady to another important actor, Henry Neville. Her successes mounted and she was courted by many eligible young men, including one who rapidly secured her heart. Arthur Lewis, a rich linen-draper, was unusually cosmopolitan and artistic; he knew France and Italy, had studied their treasures, music and literature, and was described by George du Maurier as 'certainly a princely fellow'.[2]

At the time of meeting Kate, Lewis lived in a beautiful house with an equally beautiful garden, Moray Lodge on Campden Hill. His 'bachelor evenings' were a magnet for artists and the aristocratic intelligentsia, and he created the United Arts Club, which later became the Arts Club in Hanover Square. He was tall, attractive, with a most appealing personality – *and* very rich – and he fell deeply in love with the eldest Miss Terry.

From Kate's point of view, the arrival of disgraced sister Nelly into the family home at this moment was the worst timing possible. Kate had inherited her mother's conventional streak, and despite her notable success she longed for the security of a 'good' marriage, to Arthur whom she loved and for whom she would leave the theatre without a single qualm. Her immediate fear concerned her strait-laced future mother-in-law, not well disposed to actresses, who might hear of Nelly's downfall and forbid her own union. Whether Mrs Lewis heard or not, she was mollified by Kate's behaviour and charm of manner and, when the time came, gave her blessing. Meanwhile, at Stanhope Street, Nelly was angry, Kate tight-lipped, and the two sisters barely spoke.

A diversion for the troubled family appeared in the shape of Lewis Carroll, now not only the author of the best-selling *Alice in Wonderland* but also a keen amateur photographer. He soon obtained permission to record the Terrys, though three were absent – young Ben in Australia, George, presumably at his carpentry work, and baby Fred, possibly in one of his tantrums. Fred's temper throughout his life was monumental.

The results were rather dreadful, for Carroll was no Julia Cameron. He spent three days with the family, taking solo portraits and various brothers and sisters together, then one grand group against the dreary brick wall and doorway of the house. An air of gloom hangs over them, particularly the younger children, with Polly and Floss looking unutterably miserable; in the centre stand two quite stout, plain women, wearing smiles which seem out of place. It is hard to believe that they are the ravishing Ellen and Kate of legend. Is the camera lying? Or has legend grown with the years, as legends do?

Kate continued her London triumphs in 1866 as Ben, still taking shows out on the road, persuaded Nelly to join him – to give her something to do and, perhaps, to rekindle her interest in the theatre. They probably played in the popular but pedestrian melodramas of the time; Polly went with them, helping behind the scenes, and both girls wrote regularly to their mother as they travelled from town to town. On returning home, Nelly acted in a supporting role to Kate in a play called *The Hunchback* at the Olympic, but even this taste of a glamorous London theatre seems to have left her cold.

At the end of the Olympic season, Kate travelled to Manchester to play the heroine in Dion Boucicault's new drama, *The Two Lives of Mary Leigh*. This would have been a routine engagement but for one significant fact – the villain of the piece, Rawdon Scudamore, was played by a rising young provincial actor, Henry Irving. The play was disliked by local critics though later, under a new title, *Hunted Down*, the unscrupulous Scudamore gave Irving his first breakthrough to real success in London.

It is interesting to read descriptions of the Manchester production. In Laurence Irving's biography of his grandfather (*Henry Irving: the Actor and his World*, 1951), the disappointed critics 'were, however, unanimous in their praise of Irving, whose study of Rawdon Scudamore held together the flimsy story', adding that his mastery was 'not only saving an indifferent play from failure but making it into a resounding success'.[3]

Marguerite Steen's *A Pride of Terrys* (1962) has a somewhat different slant. Kate found herself in Manchester playing opposite 'an unknown provincial actor who called himself Henry Irving, as her leading man; an association which left no agreeable impression on Kate, whose utmost experience and skill were required to cover up the uncouthness of her stage partner.'[4] So where does prejudice end and truth begin? Perhaps somewhere in between – Kate, confident and charming, but ineffectual to the play's success, and Henry, raw and not yet in command of his genius, but dynamic enough to lift the play. There is a deal of anti-Irving prejudice in most Terry writings – could this be because Ellen, the one Terry still remembered today, owed her legend to a thirty-year partnership with this supreme actor-manager?

In 1867 Kate announced her engagement to Arthur Lewis and her retirement from the stage, which caused great press and public interest. Her final performance as Juliet in *Romeo and Juliet* was greeted with sensational scenes both in the auditorium and at the stage door, Kate eventually fleeing from the front of the house to a waiting cab. This was her London farewell, though she made one last appearance in Manchester before her marriage.

It was a memorable wedding, with many beautifully dressed Terrys in attendance; a contented Sarah watched the young couple with pride in their golden future, and her younger children were ecstatic, already devoted to their new brother-in-law who had entertained them so often at Moray Lodge. Only Ben was heartsore, having given so much to Kate and having seen her achieve everything he could not, in the theatre. And Nelly? She would have been superhuman not to have felt a pang of envy, contrasting the occasion with her own sad wedding. As Kate and Arthur drove away for a real honeymoon, all that awaited her was the Queen's Theatre and her present engagement with the Alfred Wigans, which she found hard to bear.

At the Queen's, Leonora Wigan was finding Nelly hard to bear, as the nervously unhappy girl fooled and giggled incessantly on stage. She was also incapable of repose, flapping about in perpetual movement in every role she played. 'Stay still – *stay still!*' bellowed Mrs Wigan at rehearsal, without great success; she then stationed herself in a stage box for performances and hissed loudly when the giggling started. This gave Nelly a shock and had a definite effect, though the urge to fool around was never conquered in her later career.

After a series of boring parts in boring plays, Nelly was chosen for a single performance of *Katherine and Petruchio*, Garrick's 1756 mutilation of *The Taming of the Shrew*. It must have been extremely short as two farces were also on the bill. The part of Petruchio was to be taken by Mr Henry Irving, and Katherine by Mrs G.F. Watts, a formal style which greatly annoyed Nelly. Although it should have been a momentous occasion, it was not, for neither of them played well. Irving was considered too much 'the rapacious brigand',[5] Nelly, in Irving's view, too frivolous. He simply could not understand her disinterest in the theatre, after a theatrical childhood and upbringing that he would have given the world to have enjoyed. It was possibly the worst moment for them to meet and work together; he thought her natural charm was her only asset, and she found him stiff and self-conscious, his talent imprisoned and unable to flower. The performance over, they gave each other no further thought.

Nelly reached crisis point during the next production, unpromisingly titled *The Household Fairy*, and one day, without a word to anyone, she simply walked out of the Queen's Theatre and out of theatrical life. She went straight to Baker Street and Edward Godwin, which suggests that their liaison had continued throughout the previous months, though unknown to the family. Poor Ben and Sarah – they must have become frantic with worry as the days passed with no word from Nelly or the many friends they contacted. In desperation they even sent a message to the Prinseps, just in case. . . . Then the police were alerted.

Shortly after, in a moment of high melodrama, Ben was called to the morgue to identify the body of a young woman drowned in the Thames. Tall and fair, she was unnervingly similar to Nelly but was discovered to be a commercial traveller's wife who had committed suicide. Nelly herself, in

Hertfordshire with Godwin, heard of this and of her parents' anguish; thinking of others for the first time, she hurried immediately to Stanhope Street and an emotional reunion. But, of necessity, it was a temporary coming-together; she had made her bold choice and, in 1868, her mode of life was quite beyond the pale.

She returned to Hertfordshire, happy with Godwin and their mutual love, and happy too to lead a country life. Did she begin to realise her isolation from her family and all she had known? Her *Memoirs* are silent on this entire episode. Later that year, Kate's first daughter was born in lovely Moray Lodge and family gatherings were jubilant, the younger Terrys thrilled with their new tiny niece. Everyone was there, save one – who was presumably never mentioned.

# THE RETURN

Mackery End in Hertfordshire was the setting for Nelly's impulsive, idealised dream of real life. There were no thoughts or regrets for the theatre in her love for Godwin and the beauty of the countryside; she was perfectly happy to wander and bask in her surroundings, waiting for his return from his London office each evening. But the little matter of running a house and providing edible meals at regular intervals was beyond her. A young village girl was brought in to help but this effort at responsibility turned out to be the blind leading the blind. And there was a further complication – Nelly was pregnant.

Godwin now had an office in Albany Street, was a Fellow of the Royal Institute of British Architects and busily active in the Architectural Association and Archaeological Society. He worked long hours in London and also travelled for the Society, so Nelly was often alone for days at a time. It is not difficult to imagine the situation, irritation creeping in as their incompatible expectations and priorities became increasingly clear.

Godwin was away when their daughter Edith (always Edy) was born in December 1869. Fortunately, Nelly had a good neighbour, Dr Rumball, who came to her aid, and her friendship with him, and most particularly with his wife, would be an important element in her future. Edy's birth signalled the fulfilment of Godwin's promise to build a house for his unorthodox family, at the boundary of Harpenden Common, a charming house named Fallows Green. Nelly was happy there, and presumably Godwin too with the introduction of a diligent nursemaid (a Rumball relative) whom they called Bo. She took charge of Edy and probably helped to keep household affairs in better order. Godwin's hard work and financial success was at last yielding its reward.

In this home of her own, Nell (no longer childish Nelly) achieved the decorative taste she had learned from her architect-mentor. The house had minimum ornament; she dressed in loose linen smocks and little Edy was soon put into kimonos. She preferred earthenware pottery to china, though a concession was made to a willow-pattern service given by Godwin's great friend, Whistler, who also provided the kimonos. Everything was as un-Victorian as imaginable, more Greco-Japanese than European; Godwin's extraordinary vision converted Nell into an exceedingly early 'hippie'.

And it suited her, giving rein to the unconventional streak, the thoughtlessness, the tendency to wild behaviour. Her early life is rich in these characteristics, shown delightfully in the farcical boys she played with such gusto in childhood, traits which her father recognised at once. How could she become so completely the grand, staid image of later years, as regal, in her theatrical ambience, as Victoria herself on the throne? It is a mystery, but only one of many contradictions in her character.

In 1872 the family was complete, with the arrival of Ted, the future Edward Gordon —, the surname not yet chosen (it would be, years later on a sudden whim, a rare appearance of that same hippie quality in Nell, for she was by then a revered icon of the English stage). Ted's birth came at a time of tension in the still ill-run household, but this was soothed by Godwin with a holiday in France which gave Nell her first sight of another country. It was an inspired choice; he was free from unremitting work, she had no responsibilities, no shopping, cooking, housekeeping, and with the nursemaid in charge of the children. She floated gracefully through cathedrals, villages and the countryside of France, a perfect companion for this man of aesthetic taste and vision, and they recaptured something of their past devotion.

Their return to Fallows Green brought cold reality and a mixture of good fortune and disaster. The friendly country doctor Rumball had died, leaving his widow to run his small private asylum for the comparatively harmless deranged. She could not have been less suited to the task and her charges escaped with such regularity that she was forced to close down the little hospital. She was a kind woman, fond of Nell and longing to be of help, and soon she was installed as 'companion', a position she held for the next thirty years.

Her loyal service and friendship were a great boon to Nell but, unfortunately, she too was unbusinesslike. Godwin provided regular money for all household bills and the mortgage payments and left for his work, imagining that all was well.

Instead, presents and clothes were bought for the children, for Boo (Mrs Rumball) and for Bo, the nursemaid, and the debts piled up. It could not go on indefinitely – the bailiffs arrived, Godwin discovered the chaos and was furious, and there seemed no way out of an abominable mess.

The immediate resolution, in an often repeated story, has an element of comic opera to it. Nell was evidently in a lane, with the children in the pony-cart, when over the hedge leapt a huntsman in pink. It was none other than her old friend and admirer, Charles Reade. Stunned amazement! There was an affectionate reunion and, without a moment's pause, Reade offered Nell the perfect part in his latest play. She refused – then, with the bailiffs in mind, said 'Yes, for forty pounds a week'[1] (the top salary for an established star). Reade stared in disbelief, remembering her failures with the Wigans – and gave in. Thus, we must believe, Ellen Terry returned to the theatre.

As it turned out, Reade had been economical with the truth, having already engaged another actress, Mrs John Wood, for the same role. But he knew that she would play for a limited time, owing to a further engagement, and Nell seemed to be the ideal replacement. He had also neglected to mention that his play, *The Wandering Heir*, had failed dismally on a provincial tour; for a man with a true theatrical 'eye' and great skill in the direction of actors, he was an appalling playwright.

Godwin, meanwhile, must have made satisfactory arrangements with bailiffs and Hertfordshire creditors as his family and furniture remained at Fallows Green. In the winter of 1873 they moved to a small house near Gordon Square in Bloomsbury, taking minimum belongings and the ubiquitous Boo and Bo. All their main possessions stayed in the country and Godwin must have been hard pressed to maintain two houses.

It was a bad time for him as he had few, if any, commissions. Nell, while waiting for Mrs Wood to finish her contract, took a short engagement in Liverpool, leaving Godwin to paint the almost unfurnished house in Taviton Street and keep an eye on his children. Edy and Ted were a difficult pair; unbelievably spoiled by Nell, their conceit was boundless and Edy's aggressive nature would dog her all her life. Boo and Bo seem to have echoed the children's mother and given in to everything.

The day after Nell's twenty-seventh birthday, 28
February 1874, marked her return to the London
stage, and she was not only remembered by a loyal
public but given a resounding welcome. The critics
were full of praise for her performance though no
one liked the play, and eventually it was taken off,
only to be replaced by one of 'Reade's ancient pot-
boilers',[2] with Nell again in the leading role. Even
her charm could not save this from early closure,
whereupon Reade, so sure he was always right and
the public wrong, rehearsed *The Wandering Heir* and
took it out on another tour. During these ups and
mainly downs, Nell's star salary was severely cut.

There is no record of the Terry clan supporting
Nell's successful return, for Ben was working as
always, and Polly and Floss, with Sarah in constant
attendance, were also making promising stage
appearances. Polly in particular – now Miss Marion
Terry – showed every sign of an exceptional acting
talent and the fact that she was fast becoming a
genuine beauty was no disadvantage. They were all
caught up in their own lives and work but must have
read Nell's glowing reviews with pleasure and
satisfaction. Godwin, marooned in Taviton Street
with virtually no work of his own, became

interested in a publication, *Women and Work*, which championed the neglected cause of women architects. He was nearing the completion of a book, *The Architecture and Costume of Shakespeare's Plays*, but he needed company and stimulation. The magazine's editor, Miss Emily Faithful, had gathered together a group of dedicated women, one of whom was an attractive, quiet girl, Beatrice Phillips. Godwin gravitated towards her immediately; he was not unaware of his personal magnetism, and the beguiled Beatrice was also an awe-struck devotee of his professional achievements. The inevitable entanglement already existed when Nell returned to London.

This must have been a shock to her, but she faced a more immediate problem – bailiffs again on the doorstep. This time they stripped the sparse house, leaving only the straw-matting which covered the floors and a vast and incongruous statue of the Venus de Milo in the main living room. Godwin was powerless to right the situation and Nell, for once assuming responsibility, removed Edy, Ted, Boo and Bo to Fallows Green, presumably with some financial assistance on which to live. She returned to Taviton Street to kick her heels, for there was no engagement in view, and to encourage Godwin to finish his long book. It was a bleak and miserable time.

Fate stepped in, in the person of tiny Marie Wilton of Bristol days. Her highly successful career in comedy had led to marriage with the equally successful Squire Bancroft, actor-manager of the Prince of Wales Theatre, London, where the main fare was comedy interspersed with indifferent melodrama. The Bancrofts' profits were so good that they planned a lavish production of *The Merchant of Venice*, casting it from within their company with the well-known Charles Coghlan as Shylock. All that now remained was to find a Portia – even Marie knew it was not her part. So there they stood in the bare room, the tiny and tall actresses under the looming Venus; the offer was made and gratefully accepted, whereupon Marie Bancroft put the icing on the cake with, 'And Mr Godwin will be asked to control the artistic direction'.[3]

It was almost too good to be true, this first major theatrical opportunity for them both. Godwin's originality created Venetian scenes of beauty and style with imaginative use of colour and light, and

Nell, dressed in his marvellous designs, her charm and swift grace at their most appealing, swept all before her. Everyone was at her feet, writers, poets, musicians, and especially painters – she was the darling of the Pre-Raphaelites, their ideal, with one exception: George Frederick Watts, safely at home with the Prinseps.

An actor who came quietly to see and admire her Portia was Henry Irving. He was already established at the Lyceum, under the Bateman management, and creating some thrilling sensations of his own. He found it difficult to equate this graceful, effortless woman with the careless, undisciplined girl who had played Katherine to his Petruchio eight years earlier. But he made no immediate contact, simply remembering a performance filled with warmth and charm.

This beautiful production with its jewel-like Portia should have delighted audiences for many months, but it failed and closed after a short run. Blame has always been laid on poor Charles Coghlan, not the right actor for Shylock, whose nerves caused him to play badly and eventually to go to pieces. But why was he not replaced by someone more suitable? Why was such an admired and expensive décor and costuming thrown into a warehouse to moulder away? It seems incomprehensible and a ludicrous waste for the Bancroft management, but it happened, and back came the tatty but popular comedies and melodramas. Nell stayed with the company, playing in everything; she was well aware of her nonsensical roles but she needed work, a steady salary and that most important stage ingredient, constant practice.

The years 1875–6 were of vital importance to the emergent Ellen Terry. Her dwindling life with Godwin ended with his departure and subsequent marriage to Beatrice Phillips, and the dissolution of her own marriage to Watts, arranged by the indefatigable Mrs Prinsep, freed her at last from her early folly. Though Ben and Sarah had never ceased to love her, the parting with Godwin heralded the complete reunion of the Terry family, which now included Edy and Ted. Only Kate Lewis at Moray Lodge stood apart; her mode of life and the educational advantages she could give her children created an unbridgeable gulf with her sister's unorthodoxy. Luckily, they both seem to have understood and accepted this without worry or loss of sleep.

Ellen aged nine, in 1856 (by courtesy of The National Trust, Smallhythe Place/photograph Ian Pooley).

The Terry family minus young Ben, George and baby Fred, photographed by Lewis Carroll, *c.* 1862. Nelly and Kate are standing in the centre (by courtesy of The National Trust, Smallhythe Place/photograph Ian Pooley).

Ellen as Alice from a painting by George Frederic Watts, 1865 (by courtesy of the National Portrait Gallery, London).

Edy, Ellen and Ted, *c.* 1883 (by courtesy of The National Trust, Smallhythe Place/photograph Ian Pooley).

Ellen as Ophelia and Henry Irving as Hamlet in 1878 (© National Trust Photographic
Library/John Hammond).

Ellen as Beatrice in *Much Ado About Nothing* (image supplied by Getty Images).

Marion Terry (Mander and
Mitchenson).

Ellen as Lady Macbeth, 1888, wearing the remarkable dress and cloak covered with green beetle wings (image supplied by Getty Images).

Henry Irving as Shylock in *The Merchant of Venice* (image supplied by Getty Images).

Ellen's last home, Smallhythe Place in Kent (© National Trust Photographic Library/Don Carr).

Ellen Terry and James Carew looking at a book in the dining room at Smallhythe Place, in 1907 just after their marriage (© National Trust Photographic Library/John Hammond).

A previously unpublished picture of Ellen Terry in later life (by kind permission of Sir John Gielgud).

While Ellen, at the Prince of Wales, established herself as a leading member of her profession, Marion was on her way to a similar position at the Strand Theatre. Henry Irving, at the Lyceum, had already amazed the public with Mathias in *The Bells, Eugène Aram, Charles I, Richelieu*, and in Shakespeare, a vaunted *Hamlet* and a more critically received *Macbeth* and *Othello*. Ellen had seen his first *Hamlet* – 'the one and only Hamlet of her life'[4] – and would later see his greater performance which 'swept her away'.[5]

After Othello, a part he never fully conquered, Irving played King Philip of Spain in the play *Queen Mary*, by Tennyson. Ellen was there, having been taken to the Lyceum by Charles Coghlan, who was still with the Bancroft company and quite recovered from Shylock. They were enthralled, Ellen later writing of Irving's performance, 'he never did anything better to the day of his death'.[6] She, meanwhile, severed her connection with the Bancrofts, moving to the John Hare management at the Court Theatre, Sloane Square, where she scored a tremendous personal success in the title role of *Olivia*, W.G. Wills' adaptation of *The Vicar of Wakefield*. The role was written for her – a perfect Ellen Terry vehicle – and critics and the public were enslaved.

As if this was not sufficient Terry glory, Marion, now at the Haymarket, enchanted the public and critics in W.S. Gilbert's amusingly titled *Dan'l Druce, Blacksmith*. It was a significant success which led, in 1877, to the flowering of this most original actress in another Gilbert play, *Engaged*. Comedy, to the late Victorians, meant broad, crude interpretation with nothing left to the imagination, and along came Marion with the very first 'deadpan throwaways'. Today, this is still thought, mistakenly, to be an American invention. The public, at first confused, was soon helpless with laughter at her novel approach and immaculate timing, which signalled the change from old-style to modern comedy. Marion, the only Terry who fully embraced 'new' theatre writing, was born for the elegance and wit of Oscar Wilde.

Acting with Marion at the Haymarket was the strikingly handsome Johnston Forbes-Robertson, and at the Court with Ellen a burly actor, Charles Wardell, whose stage name was Kelly. They were opposites, Kelly muscular and sexy, Forbes-Robertson poetically romantic with talent as a painter, and both were in love with Ellen. She was alone, with two children to support, and a new husband seemed a wise idea, if not an actual necessity. Which was it to be? Ellen never pretended, even to herself, that she was in love with the men she married – she was just a little careless in her choice.

The family hoped that Forbes-Robertson would soon enter their ranks; Ben, in particular, had sized Kelly up in a moment and knew that the bottle would be his downfall. But Kelly it was. He married Ellen quietly one morning during the run of *Olivia*, and by the evening he arrived on stage blissfully drunk. Her reaction has not been recorded, but Forbes-Robertson, coming to the Court at the end of his own performance, left in disgust.

Though it was an ill-fated marriage lasting only five years, Kelly, to his credit, was a kind stepfather, much liked by Edy. She, in her militant way, hated her own father, Godwin, while fat little Ted – with so much of his father's taste and talent dormant in him – resented Kelly and the name Wardell, briefly thrust upon them. At this time the children seem to have lived, with helpers, in a cottage at Hampton Court, beside Bushey Park. Ted later recalled visits to the palace, wandering through the state rooms and gardens but never accompanied by their mother.

Mr and Mrs Wardell lived in Longridge Road, Earl's Court, and, when not acting in London, went out on provincial tours. On one of these, Ellen played her first Beatrice, her ideal role, and as Benedick, Kelly gave such a splendid performance that she always preferred it to any other, including Irving's. Among much else, Ellen played Sheridan's Lady Teazle and, by all accounts, not very well. Perhaps she was the wrong sister, for surely Marion would have been perfect casting. But *Olivia* continued to carry all before her, and it was while she reigned at the Court Theatre that Ellen received a visitor.

It was Henry Irving who arrived at Longridge Road after tentative letters about date and time. There is amusement and charm in this encounter of the two theatrical heavyweights; when Henry left, Ellen was still not sure whether or not he had really asked her to join him at the Lyceum. Further letters were exchanged and certainty established. Contrary to her choice of husbands, Ellen made no mistake over this. Her perennial legend was about to begin.

# SIX

# HENRY

George Bernard Shaw, who spent many years criticising Henry Irving's every move, wrote this tribute when the great actor was safely dead:

> Those who understand the art of the theatre and knew his limitations could challenge him on every point except one, and that was his eminence. Even to call him eminent belittled his achievement: he was pre-eminent. He was not pre-eminent for this, that or the other talent or faculty: his pre-eminence was abstract and positive: a quality in itself and in himself so powerful that it carried him to Westminster Abbey.[1]

What would Henry have made of this? He had always referred to his tormentor as 'Pshaw!', a nicely judged put-down of the budding Irish wizard, so this final volte face might have struck an alarming note. And Ellen – what did *she* think on reading this? Her long, somewhat arch correspondence with

Shaw culminated in his claim to have 'destroyed Ellen Terry's belief in Irving';[2] a strange boast from a man of such intelligence and wit. Perhaps he was caught between his safely distant flirtation and his gift for trouble-making, with a healthy dash of jealousy — Shaw, like Dickens, was always an actor *manqué*.

Henry Irving was born John Henry Brodribb, ... Somerset in 1838; an energetic country boy who inherited from his Cornish mother (née Behenna) height, an elegant bearing and long, thin legs. These legs, earning him the nickname Spindleshanks and causing much self-consciousness, would become a wonderfully visual stage attribute in his career. A less happy feature was his boyhood stammer, on which he worked tirelessly, to its completely successful eradication.

His first ten years were spent in Cornwall where he attended a dame school, becoming devoted to books and the recitation and declamation of exciting passages, mingled with enjoyable childish naughtiness with his school friends. Transferred to the City of London in 1848, where his parents' unsettled life had taken them, he was enrolled at the City Commercial School, near the George and

Vulture Inn, the haunt of Dickens' Mr Pickwick and the effervescent Sam Weller.

The kindly Dr Pinches, his headmaster, noted the imaginative, histrionic streak in this hard-working boy and gave him, on speech days, his first opportunities of public performance. These were seized gratefully, as Johnnie (as he then was) was denied encouragement at home. His father seemed quietly pleased by his son's independent interests but it was his mother, a devout Methodist, who ruled the roost. Performance of any kind was anathema to her; she believed such activity to be a sign of everlasting damnation and, to the end of her life, she never forgave Irving his choice of career: an abiding sadness to him.

His choice was made at the age of twelve, when his father took him to Sadler's Wells to see Samuel Phelps play Hamlet – an unforgettable experience. But first, after leaving school, he became a junior clerk in a City legal firm, and later in Thacker, Spink & Co., an East India Merchants company, making many friends but little money. When he could, he visited Sadler's Wells, reading every play beforehand and becoming almost word-perfect; his feeling for the theatre was a real passion.

During these City years he read and studied, attended elocution schools, acted with amateur groups and, always eagle-eyed, watched people in daily life; much was noted and stored away for future interpretation. In 1856 an uncle gave him £100 and Johnnie went out to do a little shopping. All actors at that time had to provide their own costumes and props and he hired doublet and hose, shoes with rosettes and a feathered hat, and bought two fine swords and a dagger, several wigs, buckles, lace and paste jewellery. Now equipped, he entered his name for the part of Romeo in an amateur performance at the Royal Soho Theatre, to take place on 11 August. He was accepted and had to pay three guineas for the privilege.

How would he style himself? He was already professional enough to know that Brodribb was not the name for a playbill, but . . . what should it be? Various ideas were whittled down to two, Baringtone and Irving; the first an amalgam of a great City name with Buckstone, a leading comedian of the day, and the second from Edward Irving, the eloquent evangelist (perhaps for his mother?) and Washington Irving, whose stories he had loved as a boy. Finally, he chose Irving –

Baringtone, tried out on many pieces of paper, looked altogether too pompous – and on the Royal Soho Theatre bill announcing '*Romeo and Juliet* for One Night Only', the public read the legend 'First Appearance of Mr Irving as Romeo'.

It is an amusing bill to read today. The entire cast is there, in tiny print; all the male characters, then, at the end, only penultimate to 'The Nurse', is 'Juliet – Mrs Henderson'. Who was she? Could she act? Did she, years later, sit in the Lyceum to applaud her raw, eighteen-year-old Romeo in his eminence? No one will ever know; she is a ghost of theatrical history.

This stage baptism as Romeo gave Henry (no longer Johnnie) the spur he needed. He secured an engagement with the Stock Company of Sunderland, told his parents of his plans and gave in his notice at Thacker, Spink & Co. He was virtually penniless but buoyed up by determined ambition and the affectionate encouragement of friends. He left behind a souvenir, the name Brodribb carved on his office desk; the same desk was occupied years later by another young man longing to escape into the theatre – A.E. Matthews, a delightful character actor beloved by all.

For twelve years Henry toiled in the provinces, in a hard, often miserable apprenticeship that would have broken most men – at Sunderland, Edinburgh, Glasgow, Manchester, playing in everything, having to dance and sing and receive occasional applause but more frequently cat-calls. He was stiff and self-conscious, his voice not always under control, but critics noted his subtly exact make-up, dress and 'business' in all he attempted. Some early success came in farce, when his ability to get 'laughs' branded him as a low comedian. And he scored a definite hit as Venoma the Spiteful Fairy in the *Sleeping Beauty* pantomime in Edinburgh!

A short season at Dublin's disreputable Queen's Theatre followed, where he replaced the dismissed juvenile lead, one George Vincent, darling of the public hooligan element. The disgruntled Vincent organised a huge *claque* of alarming roughness which shrieked and howled throughout Henry's every appearance; somehow he endured it for two long weeks until, finally, the management brought in the police, who fought and ejected the louts. In his last week he gained applause and a certain respect, for he had weathered an onslaught that few actors receive – and he had learned a great deal.

In 1860, while Kate Terry was making her mark as Cordelia with the Keans in London and Ellen played Prince Arthur in their *King John*, Henry Irving was still an impoverished twenty-two-year-old in Manchester. There would be another six years of dogged work in wretched parts, with a single threadbare suit and the humiliation of having to borrow the occasional half-crown from fellow actors for food after a performance. In one year he made only £75.

But there were compensations. He was universally popular, making staunch friends for the rest of his life; supporting the famous American actor, Edwin Booth, whom he greatly admired in his Manchester season; and falling in love with the enchanting young actress, Nellie Moore. His penury made a declaration impossible but he longed for the day when he might win her. She had already appeared with success in London and she returned there, leaving Henry, near despair, in the never-ending provinces.

Fate beckoned, and not before time. In 1866, in Liverpool without work but going regularly to the stage door in the hope of letters, he received the lifeline he needed. The irascible Irish playwright,

Dion Boucicault, wrote to offer him the part of the villainous Rawdon Scudamore in his new play. Henry threw himself into it, creating his first complete critical success and, in the process, encountering the Terry family in the shape of Kate, who was unimpressed.

There seems to have been a certain theatrical snobbery in both Kate and Ellen towards actors who lacked their theatre background. Perhaps understandably, they had no conception of the dedicated struggle of many who came later to the stage, often against much opposition. Irving, with his early lack of confidence and ease, was considered uncouth and without talent, unworthy of any further interest. The fact that his passion for the theatre, through every adversity, was far greater than theirs, quite passed them by.

Scudamore in *Hunted Down* brought Henry to London; to a most distinguished first night audience with, in a specially given stall, Mr Blackwell of Thacker, Spink & Co. One of Irving's lifelong characteristics was never to forget early friends and colleagues. At the first interval, George Eliot, in a box with G.H. Lewes, said, 'What do you think of him?' Lewes replied, 'In twenty years he will be at the head of the English stage.' The novelist murmured, 'He is there, I think, already.'

But not quite. Several more years of acting and stage management on a pittance would be endured before his meeting with the eccentric American impresario, Hezekiah Bateman, lessee of the Royal ‸‸‸ Theatre. During these years he met and worked with the estranged Mrs G.F. Watts, Ellen a failed Katherine to his failed Petruchio. Neither could understand the other – Ellen careless, disillusioned with Watts, in love with Godwin, and Henry, so dedicated and hard-working that he frightened her. It was an unedifying engagement for them both.

Also during these years, tragedy came to Henry – perhaps the greatest of his life – the death of Nellie Moore. They had met again in London but something was wrong, something had come between them which he did not understand. Their tenuous liaison over, Henry found himself cast as Bill Sykes in a forthcoming production of *Oliver Twist*, with his beloved Nellie as Nancy. Both had great success, Nellie being hailed as the most promising young actress of the time. She was suddenly taken ill and left the cast; Henry, deeply worried, went to her house near Soho Square and was told that she had scarlet fever. A few days later, carrying a bunch of violets, he called again – the blinds were drawn and he was told of her death. There were disquieting rumours, a man he knew was involved and there were hints of an 'injury' to Nellie. Did Henry suspect the unwanted result of seduction and the Victorian backstreet barbarity which so often caused early death? His love for Nellie and hatred for the unnamed man lasted until his own death in 1905 in Bradford, when two small portraits, pasted back to back, were found in his pocket-book – of Nellie and himself.

Work was the panacea, and the contract he signed in 1871 with the ebullient, slightly crazy H.L. Bateman brought his goal within sight. The Bateman family, including three acting daughters much touted by their determined father, was kindness itself to Irving at a depressing time in his private life. And at the Lyceum, the sensation of *The Bells*, under Henry's direction, heralded his progress towards the Shakespeare tragedies he imagined in perfectly designed productions.

His innovative *Hamlet* led the way in 1875, followed too quickly by the sudden death of impresario/manager Bateman, after which the Lyceum reins were taken up by his efficient and experienced widow. Henry's climb to the heights continued, but not without setbacks – the semi-failure of the experimental *Macbeth* and *Othello*, recouped by his Philip of Spain in Tennyson's *Queen Mary* and a revival of W.G Wills' *Charles I*. The productions flowed on while, in the same year, Ellen enchanted London as the Bancrofts' Portia and Kate, with her husband and children, adorned Moray Lodge. Soon Ellen would also grace a Wills' play when *Olivia* ran for several seasons at the Court Theatre, her success and superlative reviews not unnoticed by the Lyceum's leading actor.

Thus, the new Mrs Wardell received the visit and offer at Longridge Road and, on 30 December 1878, playing Ophelia to Irving's Hamlet, a rare theatrical partnership was born.

# SEVEN

# THE LYCEUM

The Bateman years were over and Henry Irving was now the lessee of the Lyceum Theatre; one of his first acts as actor-manager was the acquisition of Ellen Terry as leading lady. The transfer of power had been effected with dignity and ease, in great measure due to the wisdom and generosity of Mrs Bateman. An embarrassing situation had arisen when her daughter, Isabel, the current leading actress, had fallen hopelessly in love with Henry, a condition she was quite unable to conceal. This, added to the fact that her talent was inadequate, forced him to write to her mother, stating that he must have a player of greater stature for future seasons.

Mrs Bateman understood and, fortunately, was herself interested in taking over and restoring the old Sadler's Wells Theatre. Their exchange of letters was both businesslike and affectionate, for there was much fondness between them and gratitude for all that had been achieved. Henry's many friends helped him with initial finance while Mrs Bateman went to work on the Wells, and Isabel, who had always preferred religion to the theatre, eventually entered her chosen world as a nun. Ellen, unaware of this background to her engagement, arrived at the Lyceum like a breath of fresh air.

She watched Henry direct his new production of *Hamlet* with amazement, for this was her first sight of meticulously concentrated rehearsal where no detail or nuance was overlooked. But as time passed she became worried, for Irving never rehearsed any scenes with her. In her *Memoirs* she writes of tackling him: 'I am very nervous about my first appearance with you. Couldn't we rehearse *our* scenes?' And he replied, the manager in ascendancy over the actor, '*We* shall be all right, but we are not going to run the risk of being bottled up by a gas-man or a fiddler.'[1] She adds that he was taking a band rehearsal at the time.

They obviously did rehearse before the opening night but she felt uncertain and unhappy, playing, as she thought, badly and leaving the theatre before the curtain calls to drive up and down the Embankment in deep depression. Henry was also not at his best, as was habitual to him on first nights throughout his career. They both suffered from crippling nerves on these occasions and, for Ellen, this would get worse when her memory began to fail. But for Ophelia she need not have worried; her charm was as potent as ever, and the critics were at her feet.

Several Terry biographers – all women – assert at this point that Henry, too, was not only at her feet but in her bed. Various accounts reach a level of romantic fiction worthy of Elinor Glyn; there is even a risible moment when Ellen, like Miss Glyn in a well-known photograph, reclines on a bearskin rug! All this is stoutly disclaimed by Laurence Irving, Roger Manvell and Ellen's niece, Olive, Florence's daughter. For Ellen's female chroniclers, this burning issue ignores the presence of burly Wardell and sits ill with their denigration of Irving's single-minded concentration and self-absorbed egotism which they ceaselessly harp upon.

They also minimise the real relationship, one of devotion, which illuminated their theatre partnership. Henry gained much help from Ellen's straightforward answers to his worries about his 'gait', his vocal mannerisms and his still-apparent unease in certain roles. Though slightly in awe of him, she made valuable suggestions: that he discard the padding he used to disguise his long thin legs, and that, instead of standing in the wings becoming too keyed up for his entrances, he remain in his dressing-room to be called to the stage at exactly the right moment.

Irving always listened to, and profited from, the critical views of others. For his part, he coaxed Ellen out of a bad habit in a charming way. She had a tendency to shout in certain scenes and, when this happened, he stood in the wings and silently dropped a white handkerchief – the message excellently conveyed.

There was also his pleasure in the company of Ellen's Edy and Ted, sometimes on brief holidays or at the theatre. This was heightened by Henry's loss of his own two boys for, in 1878, he had become an estranged husband. After Nellie Moore's death, a mild friendship with Surgeon-General O'Callaghan's daughter, Florence, developed into something more. She had been captivated by his stage performances and had quite determined to marry him. He was flattered (despite the disdain of her family, which naturally lessened with his increasing success) but unfortunately blind to a waspish dominance in Florence's character, already just discernible.

They married in July 1869, Henry longing for secure domestic happiness, Florence quickly irked by the demands of his profession and especially by his actor friends. The birth of a son the following year thrilled his father to the core but Florence continued as spiky as ever, to the point when Irving was forced to take bachelor rooms in Mount Street for an attempt at peace of mind. He was allowed to see his son once each fortnight.

At the time of his meeting with H.L. Bateman and the Lyceum contract, Florence came to him, entreating his return and promising an end to ill-temper and a guard on her tongue. It was all he wished for and, though with little money from ceaseless work, he took a three-year lease on a house in West Brompton. There were a few weeks of compatibility before Florence's sharp-tongued discontent began again. She was pregnant when Henry was caught up with preparation for the first production of *The Bells*; she may have felt neglected as he worked daily, often till late at night, when he sometimes stayed with the Bateman family rather than return to anger and resentment.

For the opening performance he arranged that two close friends should accompany Florence to the stage box. It was perhaps the most sensational first night since the days of Edmund Kean and the ovation for the melodramatic tragedy continued long after the curtain on Mathias's death. It was followed by *Pickwick*, in which Irving's Jingle demonstrated his versatility as a witty comedian. (In the 1940s Laurence Olivier may well have had Irving in mind when he amazed us as *Oedipus*, followed by Mr Puff in *The Critic*.)

Jingle received further ovations on 25 November 1871 and Henry was bombarded by a host of excited visitors to his dressing-room. Florence sat in a brougham at the stage door, impatient and irritable; the accompanying friends had already gone home to arrange the final touches to the celebratory dinner they were giving for Henry and his wife. Eventually he appeared and climbed into the cab beside her.

There was champagne, laughter and eulogy for the evening's triumph from the exhilarated dinner party guests, all save one whose attitude 'let in a cold draught of sceptical ill-humour', and who feared 'that her husband might be boring the company'.[2] As they returned home, a fine carriage may have passed their brougham, causing Henry to put his hand on his wife's arm, saying, 'Well, my dear, we too shall soon have our own carriage and pair!'³ Florence, consumed by jealous resentment, replied, 'Are you going on making a fool of yourself like this all your life?'⁴

They were at Hyde Park Corner. Henry asked the driver to stop; he got out without a word, walked to the Batemans' house at Kensington Gore, never returned home and never spoke to his wife again. Those few moments hardened him and brought about a lonely, much less trusting future. When his second son was born the following year, there was no invitation to the christening, nor did Henry ask for one. The separation from his boys in their early years was his greatest sadness and Florence's malice overflowed at all Lyceum first nights when she would bring the boys to the stage box and publicly mock and ridicule their father. Yet he was the family's financial support, at first from a weekly salary of £15, which was depleted by money he sent regularly to his widowed father.

From the 1871 separation, Henry knew his wife's character all too well, and knew that any breath of scandal attached to him would bring a Fury's merciless onslaught. During his long stage partnership with Ellen there was no hint of a sexual relationship or indiscretion, much as speculative gossip would have loved it, and it is only since Ellen's death that vivid allegations have appeared. While she lived . . . not a word.

Her first night nerves and depression long past, Ellen settled happily into her comfortable dressing-room and the Lyceum routine. Unlike Henry, her only responsibilities were rehearsals and performances, the ideal situation for this light-hearted woman. She was popular with everyone, causing only slight discomfort by being wildly late for every rehearsal which involved her. But Henry realised that she was quite incapable of punctuality – part of her charm? – and never said a word.

During the run of *Hamlet*, Ellen's generosity of spirit towards her stage partner shines through her *Memoirs* as she describes his ensemble direction and his own subtlety of performance; the qualities of 'strength, delicacy, distinction . . . never a touch of commonness . . . blood and breeding pervaded him . . . with a melancholy as simple as it was profound.'[5] And in a further delightful comment, 'He neglected no *coup de théâtre* to assist him, but who notices the servants when the host is present?'[6]

Ellen's Ophelia was greatly admired but, as with
all her work, there is no description of her actual
performance, only of her lovableness and all-
conquering charm, references which came to
aggravate her as she grew older. Of the year 1879
and, indeed, of her first ten years at the Lyceum, she
wrote, 'I can answer in one word: "*Work*".'[7] Ophelia
was followed by Bulwer Lytton's *Lady of Lyons*, in
which neither Ellen nor Henry played well; then by
eleven productions of which only two are still played
today, *Richard III* and *The Merchant of Venice*.

Only the first act of *Richard III* was given, for it shared
the bill with a farce called *Raising the Wind*, in which
Irving played a character, Jeremy Diddler, in full
comedic fig. Ellen's Lady Anne was presumably
charming, though there are no accounts. She was again a
radiant Portia, this time to Henry Irving's first Shylock.
This famous production was preceded by the annual
closure of the theatre from August to October, when
Ellen and her husband, Charles, toured the provinces
with their own company. Her brother George Terry
went too, as business manager, and it was in Leeds that
*Much Ado about Nothing* was produced, with Charles
proving the favourite Benedick of Ellen's Beatrice.
She later wrote, 'I never played Beatrice as well again.'[8]

# EIGHT

# THE 1880S

The 1880s were the great Lyceum years and also saw the first American and Canadian tours for Irving's company. Nor were the British provinces forgotten and Henry, unlike other managers of the time, insisted on full-scale productions travelling to every town and theatre. The cost must have been prodigious, but he knew the value of showing the company, and himself, in impeccable settings.

Ellen's 1880 tour with Charles Kelly was their last together. Their marriage, to no one's surprise, was on the rocks and, while she dazzled at the Lyceum and on tour now with Henry, poor old Kelly nursed considerable jealousy and quite a few bottles. Within five years of separation he was dying, and Ellen was summoned to his deathbed by the young woman who lived with him. Later, she made a bizarre comment on the scene: 'When I went upstairs I could not feel it was Charles, but I had the strangest wish to rehearse Juliet there by the bed on which he was lying!'[1]

*The Merchant of Venice* was prepared and produced at the end of 1879 and proved one of Irving's lasting successes, not only for Portia and the beautiful Venetian décor but for his wholly original Shylock. He had seen Venice and eastern Mediterranean Levantines as a guest on the yacht of Baroness Burdett Coutts, a great admirer, and, in place of the savage Jew of tradition, he presented an elegant, dignified, infinitely cunning portrait. Ellen tried to adapt her earlier Bancroft performance (with the turbulent Coghlan) to match this very different Shylock, but she was unable to change her reliance on feminine charm.

This drew criticism from *Blackwood's Magazine*, much to her dismay. Had she forgotten a similar criticism of her earlier performance? It had come from the old actress Fanny Kemble, accompanying Henry James, who – in the speech beginning 'You see me, Lord Bassanio, where I stand' – watched Ellen rush to the actor's side and TOUCH him! Fanny, outraged by this lapse of taste and etiquette, said that Portia must remain still *and* at a distance. James agreed; he and Ruskin were probably the only critics who were never blinded by Ellen's charms. And it so bothered her that she was still worrying about it in 1903.

This illustrates an interesting point about critics, performers and human nature in general. Ellen's personality was so strong, her charms so delightful, that no one seemed to question her ability to act – they just adored her for herself. There was virtually no criticism because she posed no threat to preconceived ideas, a comfortable state for the public. Ellen was always an eminently 'safe' performer.

Henry was eminently '*un*safe.' Apart from his mannerisms which irritated many, his talent – perhaps genius – was too great, too original, and his *was* a threatening presence. This attracted fierce, even vitriolic, criticism which sometimes spilled over into personal defamation in the press. Exceptional talent is often vilified and certainly divides opinion sharply; it may be that the immense difference between these two actors, and their perception by the public, was the linchpin of their partnership.

Ellen always maintained that every performance at the Lyceum was, for her, either pre-*Macbeth* or post-*Macbeth*, the play which was given in 1888. By all accounts, the production was a fine one, with Irving in the final scenes, in her words, 'like a great famished wolf',[2] but she, not quite Lady Macbeth, was loved as always. Only her father, old Ben, rhapsodised over her actual performance. Walter Collinson, Henry's dresser, valet and lifelong friend, has left a memento of the production much prized by his master. Ellen recounts in her *Memoirs* how Henry, perhaps mischievously, asked Walter which he thought his best part. 'Walter could not be drawn for a long time. At last he said Macbeth. This pleased Henry immensely, for he fancied himself in Macbeth . . . "It is generally conceded to be Hamlet," said Henry. "Oh, no, sir," said Walter, "Macbeth. You sweat twice as much in that".'[3]

Walter was one of a triumvirate of 'colleagues till death', with H.J. Loveday, Irving's stage manager, and Bram Stoker, his business manager. This quartet worked together with imagination, precision, and in perfect amity from 1879 to 1905, surely a remarkable example of loyalty and excellent administration. The youngest, Bram, would, of course, go on to write his famous classic after 'The Guv'nor's' death, using his sense of the theatrical to great effect.

Early in Henry's reign at the Lyceum, he ordered the cleaning and restoration of two old backstage lumber rooms; they had been, at the beginning of the 1800s, dining room and kitchen for The Sublime Society of Beefsteaks, whose tradition he was determined to revive. The dining room became beautiful, hung with pictures from Henry's growing collection – among them Clint's Edmund Kean, a head of young Napoleon and Whistler's Irving as Philip of Spain; the kitchen was modern (for 1879), with an excellent chef and cellar installed, and the merriment of the new Beefsteak began.

Politicians, lawyers, writers, painters, musicians, members of society headed by the Prince of Wales, and, always, members of Irving's company and staff enjoyed the regular post-performance champagne and brandy suppers. The occasions were mostly male, but Ellen was there as his hostess when he entertained Alexandra, the beautiful Princess of Wales, and later when he gave a birthday party for the young Princess May of Teck.

For the hundredth performance of *The Merchant of Venice*, Henry went one better. Three hundred invitations were sent out to the great and not so great, the largest group being colleagues and friends from his struggling early days. With the last curtain the stage crew went into action as Ellen and Henry (surely a monumental quick change?) received their guests in the Beefsteak room and, after a short interval, led them to the stage. In Laurence Irving's words, 'Belmont was miraculously transformed into a great scarlet and white pavilion lit by two glittering chandeliers . . . in no time at all Mr Gunter's magicians had set out the supper tables and were poised in the wings with a hot five-course supper and cool magnums of Heidsieck 1874.'[4] As a final *bonne bouche*, every guest received a gold-embossed, vellum-bound copy of the play – a theatrical evening of style.

In pre-*Macbeth* years, the first play of the September 1880 season was Dumas' *The Corsican Brothers*, Irving playing both brothers and with no female part of consequence as Ellen was still on tour with Kelly. This production heralded the arrival, as leading juvenile, of William Terriss, who was

Byronically handsome, charmingly impudent, of great courage and rather less brain. Still in his twenties, he had become an actor after a rackety life at sea; he was enormously popular with everyone, including Henry, who allowed him greater licence than anyone else. This was tested immediately when Breezy Bill (his nickname) dress-rehearsed a duel with Henry's Corsican brother. Noticing that the limelight stayed firmly on Henry, he put up his sword and said, 'Don't you think, Guv' nor, a few rays of the moon might fall on me – it shines equally, ye know, on the just and the unjust.'[5] Bill got his share of the moonlight, as he did with everything.

Ellen loved working with him; she was captivated by his stage presence and found him a most effective actor, though half the time, in Shakespearean roles, he had no idea what he was talking about. She remembered a risible moment at a rehearsal of *Much Ado* when Bill kept trying out a line, emphasising different words each time. Finally Henry said, 'Terriss, what's the meaning of that?' and the cheeky answer, 'Oh, get along, Guv'nor, *you* know!'[6] And Henry laughed and left it at that. Breezy Bill Terriss was a real life-enhancer and it was tragic that he was killed at fifty, still Byronic, stabbed by a madman at the stage door of the Adelphi.

There was another new arrival in *The Corsican Brothers*, but an unexpected one: the Chancellor of the Exchequer, Mr Gladstone. A devotee of the Lyceum, he loved going backstage and Henry suggested that he might like to join the 'supers' seated in boxes, in the Opera House scene. He could then see the action at close quarters but he *must* sit back, veiled by the box curtain. Gladstone was thrilled; he did as he was told until a particular burst of applause made him lean forward to see the cause. The audience knew him at once. 'Bravo, Gladstone!' they bellowed, and gave him an ovation of his own. Over the years he was a staunch Lyceum 'regular' and, when deafness became a problem, Henry arranged a special seat in the prompt corner. Was there ever a more stagestruck politician?

On her return from touring, Ellen's first role was Camma in *The Cup*, a too-short play by Tennyson, then Poet Laureate, and the Corsicans were forced back to pad out the bill. She wrote amusingly of the first meeting at Eaton Place when Tennyson read his play to Irving, herself, Bill, the poet's son, Hallam, her daughter Edy, aged nine and seated on Henry's knee, and Henry's lovely woolly dog, Charlie.

Tennyson, like many Victorian poets, read in a 'low, rumbling monotone',[7] but then, for the women's voices, shot up to a high key which cracked and gave way. Edy turned to look at Hallam and they burst out laughing, Henry had a broad grin on his face and Ellen was mortified. The reactions of Bill and Charlie are unknown. But the finished production 'was one of the most beautiful things that HI ever accomplished', with décor, lighting and superb costumes by Edward Godwin; the only disappointment was 'that it was all over so quickly'.[8]

The next major play was *Othello*, when Henry invited Edwin Booth, then in a miserably unpatronised season at the run-down Princess Theatre, to alternate Othello and Iago with him. Great occasions they must have been, but a mixed blessing for them both, Henry a superlative Iago but a failed Othello, Booth a good, if not great, Othello but a wretched Iago. The one constant was Ellen's Desdemona, a part she loved and in which her gifts of sincerity, trust and pathos were at their most potent. She described Henry after his last performance as the Moor: ' . . . he rolled up the clothes that he had worn . . . carefully laying one garment on top of the other, and then, half-humorously and very deliberately, said, *"Never again!"* . . . and gave a great sigh of relief.'⁹

In 1882 the most important production was *Romeo and Juliet*, though both Ellen and Henry knew they were a shade mature for their roles. He preferred the part of Mercutio but knew that Breezy Bill was no Romeo (as was proved elsewhere a few years later) so there was no help for it. After the dress rehearsal he wrote to Ellen, praising her performance, and finishing 'I have determined not to see a paper for a week – I know they'll cut me up and I don't like it'.¹⁰

They did, but marvelled at the beauty of the production, and marvelled even more when the public packed the house for twenty-four weeks. Ellen's Juliet was damned with faint praise; she herself knew she had failed, though her public was as euphoric as ever. Together they bolstered each other up during the long run and, on the hundredth night, cocking a snook at his critics, Henry gave another tented banquet on the stage. Did a memory of the first night return, with his grim-faced wife seated in her box? Luckily, he couldn't know that she went home to write in her diary: 'First night of *Romeo and Juliet* at Lyceum – jolly failure – Irving awfully funny.'[11]

Romeo, like Othello, was consigned to a warehouse, never to be revived, while comedies, melodramas, and a lovely production of *Much Ado* delighted public and ·critics alike. Beatrice and Benedick were considered incomparable, though privately Ellen found Henry too slow and heavy – pace was always of supreme importance to her. A strong repertoire was taken to America and Canada in 1883, the first of seven highly successful trans-atlantic tours; not only was there an ecstatic reception in every city, matched by New World hospitality, but, despite the huge costs, an £11,700 profit was brought home by a tired but exhilarated company. Henry now knew that tours of Britain and America could guarantee perennial Lyceum security.

The years 1884–8 saw several major productions, all successful save one, *Twelfth Night*, which was a total disaster. Unheard-of booing from pit and gallery greeted Henry's eccentrically original Malvolio, but the first night's saddest failure was Ellen's Viola. She had to play many scenes seated in a chair, in great pain from a poisoned thumb and ever-swelling arm in a sling. It was Bram Stoker's doctor brother who treated her and averted a possible amputation, but she had to leave the cast, her sister Marion taking over her role.

Marion again saved the day in Wills' *Olivia*. Irving, bereft of new dramatists and new plays, had resurrected Ellen's earlier triumph especially for her, but she again became ill during the run. However, she recorded 'the only *comfortable* first night I ever had',[12] because her own Edy and Ted were on stage in walk-on parts.

Wills adapted Goethe's *Faust* for the 1885 season. Henry, with his designer and friends, had visited Germany – medieval Rothenberg in particular – for architecture, atmosphere, and authentic furniture, costume and every type of prop. Ellen was also in the party with Edy, taking her to concerts as Edy's ambition was for a career in music, though sadly this became impossible when a permanent rheumatic condition was later diagnosed.

They returned to London and a frenzy of preparation; vast sets were constructed and an organ installed at the back of the stage. Henry, on hearing its first celestial pipings, murmured 'Mmm . . . sounds to me like an Archbishop pidd-ling'.[13] But 'this confection of lyrical melodrama and infernal pageantry', maligned by some as 'clap-trap',[14] proved the Lyceum's greatest commercial success, giving Henry immense enjoyment as a scarlet Mephistopheles and Ellen a favourite role as the Ophelia-like Marguerite.

And so to the watershed *Macbeth*, with its grand settings, effective lighting and music by Sullivan. Everyone agreed on the splendour of the production, even Irving's cruellest critics conceding that he now had far greater power and authority than in his earlier wayward attempt. But for Ellen, it was perhaps the only time she came near to actual criticism of her work. One reviewer wrote that Henry 'had persuaded himself that Lady Macbeth . . . is, in reality, the sweetest, most affectionate character that ever drew breath . . . an aesthetic Burne Jonesy, Grosvenor Gallery version . . . who roars as gently as any sucking dove.'[15] But Henry stuck to his guns and thought her wonderful.

She certainly looked wonderful in gorgeous costumes designed by her friend Alice Comyns-Carr. They fascinated Oscar Wilde, who adored Ellen and haunted the Lyceum; leaving after the first night, he quipped to friends that Lady M obviously did her shopping in Byzantium.[16] John Singer Sargent may well have thought the same when he painted her full-length portrait in the amazing green beetle-wing dress.

# NINE

# EDY AND TED

The post-*Macbeth* years were enlivened by grand-scale productions of *Henry VIII* and *King Lear*; Henry's Wolsey and Ellen's Katherine of Aragon were much praised; Ellen in Steen's description 'dissolved her audience in tears and received rapturous letters from poets and painters'.[1] *Lear* was more controversial, a first-night failure for Henry through nervous inaudibility, though Ellen, playing Cordelia at forty-five, was still adored as herself. One wonders why she did not choose either of the older daughters, Goneril or Regan, both strong, meaty parts. Perhaps their characters were too unsympathetic and therefore unappealing to her.

Before these giant plays came a French Revolution miniature, *The Dead Heart*, an 1859 melodrama by Watts Philips, rewritten by Walter Pollock for 1889. Henry played a pre-Sidney Carton character and Ellen the mother of the young

Comte St Valéry whom he saves from the guillotine. To persuade her to play this matron, Henry wrote a charmingly adroit letter which led her to comment, 'The crafty old Henry! All this was to put me in conceit with my part!'[2] What really put her in conceit was the presence of her son, Ted, as the Comte.

Ted was rather good. At seventeen he showed great promise as an actor and, during the Lyceum vacation months, went on to play Romeo, Macbeth and Hamlet with other companies. He later wrote, 'Acting these, I discovered that I was not a second Irving. Returning to the Lyceum, I discovered why',[3] a touching display of self-knowledge.

Humility and self-knowledge are not qualities usually associated with Edward Gordon Craig, the name he assumed in 1888. This came about in haphazard fashion when, with his mother, Henry, and possibly Edy, he was on holiday on the west coast of Scotland, driving past a huge dark rock out in the Atlantic. They were intrigued, asked what it was and were told Ailsa Craig. Ellen was delighted, 'What a good stage name! A pity you can't have it, Ted. I shall give it to Edy.'[4] And she did. There was a somewhat late christening ceremony in London, nineteen-year-old Edy becoming Edith Ailsa Geraldine (after her godmother Mrs Stephen Coleridge) and sixteen-year-old Ted now Edward Henry Gordon (for Irving and Lady Gordon). Craig was added by deed poll, finally settling the uncertainty of Godwin, Terry or Wardell.

With his performance in *The Dead Heart*, Ted was 'given preferment' in future Lyceum productions, 'at his mother's request'.[5] He has been described as conceited, vain and unscrupulous and he certainly used people mercilessly throughout his life. So sure was he of his talents that he was not the least crestfallen by early expulsion from his public school, Bradfield, and later from Heidelberg University. His exact misdemeanours have never been made clear.

Ellen thought him a wonderful actor and was deeply distressed when he abandoned performance for design. But this was the area of his real original talent and he became, mainly in European theatres, the pioneer of the cyclorama, the dramatic use of screens and starkly effective décor on a monumental scale. He was invariably short of money and sponged disgracefully; he fathered children all over the place, marrying once but impermanently. A turbulent affair with Isadora Duncan ended with the death of their little daughter, Deirdre, drowned in the Seine in a tragic carriage accident, while Ted continued his long liaison with a charming Italian, Elena Meo. Their two children became Ellen's particular favourites in her old age.

Despite this colourful life, Ted published books of value on his idiosyncratic, futurist view of theatre design and presentation, and founded in Florence the Goldoni School of experimental stage design. In England, the selfless Elena Meo worked tirelessly to raise finance for this project and Ellen was often the sole support of her grandchildren. Ted also published, in 1931, a rather dreadful book, *Ellen Terry and her Secret Self*, an affected, saccharine account of 'the great actress' versus 'little Nelly, the mother'. It is basically an apologia for his own neglect, but he found space for some idiotic views, including the nonsense that Shakespeare's plays are complete on the page and performance merely ruins them.

His eccentric, undependable character could not have been in greater contrast to that of his sister. Edy was the toiler, the responsible one, always there, always reliable. It was her great misfortune to seem aggressive and boorish and apparently charmless, traits from early childhood which may have been intensified by the cruel rheumatic condition which ended her musical training in Germany. She also acted at the Lyceum, for Ellen was sure of her talent, but Edy was not interested and turned instead to costume design, for which she had an exceptional gift. Her mother was often the beneficiary.

There are accounts that Edy, in her early twenties, had two heterosexual love affairs which were brought to an end by Ellen's disapproval. All that is certain is that Edy's natural feminism became more strident and her attraction towards women stronger; she met the writer Christabel Marshall, who called herself Christopher St John, and they set up house together. Later, they were joined by another woman, Clare Atwood, called Tony, and this *ménage à trois* became the part-support, part-harassment of Ellen's last years. Edy's relationship with her mother has a familiar ring; in many ways they were estranged, yet clamped together emotionally as well as literally at Ellen's final Kentish farmhouse, Smallhythe Place. After his mother's death, and aware of his own cavalier absence during her lifetime, Ted most unattractively maligned his sister and her many years of prickly devotion.

In 1892, the year of *Henry VIII* and *Lear*, Sarah Terry died and was much mourned by her large family. It was also the year when Ellen and Bernard Shaw began their roguish correspondence, Shaw undermining Irving and the Lyceum policy at every turn. His attempts to lure Ellen into new modern plays came at a time when her memory, never strong, was beginning to fail; later she would leave her lines on pieces of paper dotted about the stage or snap her fingers at the prompter and make quite audible demands for help. No member of her public ever seemed to mind.

In 1893 Oscar Wilde touched the heights with *Lady Windermere's Fan*. Beautiful, elegant Marion created a sensationally sexy Mrs Erlynne, while brother Fred appeared in Herbert Beerbohm Tree's production of *A Woman of No Importance*. But Wilde plunged to the depths and, after his arrest and public revulsion, his plays were withdrawn. He was ruined as his notorious trials progressed, ending in the irony of this 'man of the theatre' being found guilty and sentenced on 25 May 1895, the very day when Henry Irving became the first knight of the theatre. This was the recognition Henry had wanted for his slighted profession; Max Beerbohm glimpsed him in a brougham en route to Paddington and the Queen at Windsor, recalling 'the old Bohemian . . . with a look of such ruminant sly fun . . . the soul of a comedic philosopher revelling in a foolish world'.[6]

But the Lyceum was waning and in debt. Ellen played Imogen in *Cymbeline* in the following year, a great role but not enough to silence Shaw and others in their denigration of her 'unworthy parts' and Ellen's now fuelled discontent. Worse was to come. Henry suffered permanent damage from a knee injury, and a terrible fire in Southwark destroyed the scenery of forty-four productions, the flower of the Lyceum's great years – all under-insured. And Henry, on tour in Edinburgh, caught a chill, travelled to Glasgow and was struck down with pleurisy and pneumonia.

Though he continued to overwork into the new century, Irving's health was broken. Ellen visited him while he recuperated in Bournemouth in 1899; it was a difficult meeting, partly because he had been forced, financially, to relinquish the Lyceum to a syndicate, more crucially because he had nothing of merit to offer her. Fifty-two-year-old actresses are not easy to cast.

Ellen went off on tour with the actor Frank Cooper, playing Desdemona and *The Lady of Lyons* – 'unworthy parts', hissed her fans. And in no time at all, she was rumoured to be the lover of Frank Cooper. Ellen wrote to a friend, 'They marry me off to every man I act with – "She acts so naturally" they say – "it must be real" – Silly-fool-Asses!!!'[7] In 1901 there was one last Shakespeare play for her at the Lyceum – *Coriolanus*, which was greeted by a cool reception from a thin public. The syndicate and Henry were bankrupt and the receiver was called in. With Ellen, Henry played Shylock to her Portia once more on the Lyceum stage, before leaving it forever.

At this time Ellen was engaged at His Majesty's Theatre, London, playing a rollicking Mistress Page to Madge Kendal's Mistress Ford and Herbert Beerbohm Tree's Falstaff in Shakespeare's *The Merry Wives of Windsor*. Her last performance with Irving was at a charity matinée at Drury Lane in July 1903 – they were Shylock and Portia again in an emotional farewell. Henry was worn out, still touring America and England when, after playing Tennyson's *Becket* in 1905, he collapsed and died in the foyer of his Bradford hotel, his faithful Walter beside him. Although he was penniless, his last years had not been entirely unhappy; his two boys, both good writers and actors, were close to him and had a complete understanding of the past. With a charming woman, Mrs Eliza Aria, he had found loving companionship, which perhaps brought memories of his long-lost Nellie Moore and what might have been.

*T E N*

# OLD ELLEN AND
# YOUNG JACK

When Ellen gave her last performance with Henry at Drury Lane, she had taken a short lease of the Westminster Imperial Theatre, venturing unwisely into management with her unpredictable son. The choice of play, Ibsen's *The Vikings*, was disastrous, giving Ted opportunities for new expensive lighting and gargantuan décor but providing Ellen with a hopelessly unsuitable role. The family had warned of frayed tempers and failure and they were right; *Much Ado*, with Oscar Asche as Benedick, was hurried on in the hope of salvation, but even Ellen's renowned Beatrice faced half-empty houses and inevitable closure.

She at once went out on tour, hoping to recoup her losses; again she chose an unsuitable modern play, *The Good Hope*, in tandem with *Much Ado*, and again demonstrated her inability to take responsibility or gauge her public correctly. In 1905, when Henry died, she was appearing in J.M. Barrie's *Alice-Sit-By-The-Fire*, a part specially written for her. She neither liked it nor had success with it; she was essentially a Victorian player of the old school and could not adapt to modern writing.

Yet she persevered, appearing the following year as Lady Cicely in *Captain Brassbound's Conversion*, the play Shaw had long dangled under her nose in his letters. Again, this was a specially written role, containing every quirk of her personality and idiosyncrasy of performance, but again it was a disappointment. This was redeemed by one last moment of glory when, on 12 June 1906, Ellen celebrated her theatrical Golden Jubilee at Drury Lane, the stage liberally scattered with generations of acting Terrys as Ellen played the first act of her favourite Beatrice to an overwhelming reception.

It was a spectacular occasion, a mammoth matinée from noon till after six o'clock. Duse came from Italy, Réjane from France; Caruso sang – so did Gertie Millar; Gilbert's *Trial by Jury* sported dozens of famous names, with Conan Doyle a jury member; and Mrs Patrick Campbell, Beerbohm Tree, Forbes-Robertson, Irving's sons, and *Tableaux Vivants* featuring fifty leading actresses were among those honouring Ellen.

Ted was absent in Europe, which saddened his mother, but Edy was at the centre of arrangements and rehearsals, and not always happily. She had become more and more involved in Ellen's dwindling theatre work, almost her personal manager, and her brusque manner and certainty that she was always right in all situations made her extremely unpopular. The fact that she was also beginning to dominate Ellen's personal life was resented by many close friends.

This filial straitjacket was severely shaken when Ellen, at fifty-nine, became infatuated with a young German-American actor in the *Brassbound* company. James Carew from Indiana, in his mid-thirties, had determined on a theatrical career after seeing Ellen and Henry in an early Chicago performance. He came to England, worked hard, and was chosen for small parts in, first, *Man and Superman*, then *Brassbound* at the Court. He was soon a constant presence at

Ellen's King's Road house and at Smallhythe, to the irritation of Edy and her feminists. In 1907, touring America with him as her leading man, Ellen married him.

This seems to have been a situation that Carew had not anticipated but Ellen had insisted upon, for propriety's sake. The Terry family was appalled and Edy so infuriated that she severed all contact with her mother on their return to England. Her anger was probably all the greater as Ellen was her main financial support, which included her theatre costume business. Poor Carew, to be landed in such a hotbed; and with Ellen herself, it was, inevitably, a marriage of affectionate companionship, and nothing more.

It has been claimed that Ellen's marriage to Charles Kelly, when both were young, was similarly unconsummated. If this was true, it suggests that, after Edward Godwin – 'the one unforgettable, unforgotten love in her life'[1] – she craved male attention but preferred love to come to her through excessive and ardent 'lovers' correspondence' with many men, principally Bernard Shaw, and through the idolisation of her spell-bound public. This is possible and, if so, she would not have been the first fascinating, adored woman who, after a great love, found sex an unnecessary part of life.

The tensions at Smallhythe caused Ellen to become difficult to live with. After two years James Carew departed, though he always remained a kind friend. Immediately, Edy again took over her mother's affairs, rationing visits from friends and arranging far too many engagements for Ellen's age and capability. Loss of memory and poor eyesight, which had troubled Ellen for years, were ignored as Edy pushed her through performances quite unworthy of her name. Small parts in five unmemorable films were undertaken, the last as late as 1921, when Ellen was in no state to transcend the indignity.

Fortunately, she achieved a last personal distinction in lecture tours of England, America and Australia. Her subject was Shakespeare, her text written by Christopher St John, and speeches from her performances were woven into the presentation. She had success, she made much-needed money, and she enjoyed the old adrenalin of an appreciative audience; but her health gave way, a cataract operation was only partially successful, and she returned to Smallhythe to the twilight of an increasingly wandering mind.

There were compensations in the presence of her two grandchildren by Ted and Elena Meo; in a new, incomparable companion, Hilda Barnes, who kept Edy and her crew at bay; and in the award of DBE in 1925. Unfortunately, this caused fury among Ellen's closest followers – why was she not the *first* theatrical Dame, why had the American-born actress Genevieve Ward been given that honour? It was all rather foolish.

In the ever-expanding Terry family, Ellen's interest was caught by one particular great-nephew. Katie, the eldest daughter of Ellen's sister, Kate, had married Frank Gielgud, of Polish ancestry, and their third son, born in 1904, was christened Arthur John, known in the family as Jack. Ellen wrote of 'Katie's exceedingly clever boys, and one of 'em, Jack, is devoted earnestly to Ted and all his works . . . I've little strength or time or I'd see much of him.'[2]

Young Jack, who from earliest days was bound for the theatre, remembers his encounters with his great-aunt with unwavering clarity; how incredibly restless she was, even in old age; how fanatical her love of letter-writing; and how, though he cannot explain why, she mesmerised him, just as her personality must have mesmerised her audiences.

He saw her play scenes as Portia and Mistress Page and, like every critic of her time, is unable to describe the manner of her acting. But her entrances were unforgettable: 'When she came on for the Trial scene, she walked on paving stones – when she entered as Mistress Page, she walked in a meadow.'[3] These few words leave a lasting impression of the effect she could create. He also confirms the tales of Ellen's 'fooling around', chuckling through a description of Madge Kendal's apoplexy when Ellen stuck pins into Tree's Falstaff stomach to make the padding run out.

Jack, now our Sir John, thought the last years 'very sad – she was pushed around by everyone'.[4] Even so, he liked Edy very much, describing her as 'rather a high priestess' at Smallhythe, Chris St John and Clare Atwood being the overtly lesbian element. Edy had many talents, as stage designer and costumier, and as director of her own 'advanced' Pioneer Players and later Barn Players, the Sunday evening performances which were highly regarded. She had humour too, hidden under the prickly aggression; it was neatly demonstrated when Shaw, expecting to meet Ellen at her London house, read *You Never Can Tell* to an audience of two, Edy and a friend. Later, Edy's sole comment was: 'He's just the vainest flirt . . . he'd coquet with a piece of string!'[5]

Young Jack's boyish enthusiasm remains undiminished; he is still exhilarated by the imagination and originality with which Gordon Craig reinvented theatre production. He agrees with his mother's opinion of Marion Terry as *the* actress of the family, while remembering Ellen's vitality, openness and naturalness. She was a wonderfully generous woman, always trying 'to be of use'; indeed she wrote that, in her career, she hoped she had been 'a useful actress', in her view the highest achievement.

Ellen died at Smallhythe on the sunny morning of 21 July 1928, not really ill, just coming quietly to the end. Her funeral at Smallhythe church was followed by cremation at Golders Green. Then came another burst of indignation from friends and fans; her ashes were not to rest in Westminster Abbey, the honour given to Henry Irving. These blinkered people were unable to appreciate Irving's achievement for his profession and the British theatre. Ellen's memorial is in St Paul's, Covent Garden, the actors' church, among her own people. She will always be a legendary figure, but perhaps we, since 1930, have seen the best Terry of them all – young Jack, who combines the histrionic talent of great-aunt Marion with the charm of great-aunt Ellen.

# NOTES

## INTRODUCTION

1. Edward Gordon Craig, *Ellen Terry and her Secret Self*, p. 10
2. John Gielgud, *Backward Glances*, p. 124
3. Nina Auerbach, *Player in her Time*, p. 177
4. Ibid, p. 195
5. Ibid, p. 244
6. Ibid, p. 53

## CHAPTER ONE

1. Marguerite Steen, *A Pride of Terrys*, p. 118

## CHAPTER TWO

1. Christopher St John, *Ellen Terry*, p. XII
2. Steen, *A Pride of Terrys*, p. 40

## CHAPTER THREE

1. Steen, *A Pride of Terrys*, p. 84
2. Auerbach, *Player in her Time*, p. 89

## CHAPTER FOUR

1. Steen, *A Pride of Terrys*, p. 102
2. Ibid, p. 103
3. Laurence Irving, *Henry Irving, the Actor and his World*, p. 128
4. Steen, *A Pride of Terrys*, p. 107
5. Irving, *Henry Irving*, p. 147

# *N o t e s*

## CHAPTER FIVE

1. Steen, *A Pride of Terrys*, p. 135
2. Ibid, p. 138
3. Ibid, p. 139
4. Ibid, p. 143
5. Ibid
6. Ibid, p. 142

## CHAPTER SIX

1. Ned Sherrin, *Theatrical Anecdotes*, p. 126
2. Roger Manvell, *Ellen Terry*, p. 265

## CHAPTER SEVEN

1. Ellen Terry, *Memoirs*, p. 121
2. Irving, *Henry Irving*, p. 200
3. Ibid
4. Ibid
5. Terry, *Memoirs*, p. 103
6. Ibid
7. Ibid, p. 125
8. Ibid, p. 172

## CHAPTER EIGHT

1. Steen, *A Pride of Terrys*, p. 185
2. Ellen Terry, *Memoirs*, p. 232
3. Ibid, p. 141
4. Irving, *Henry Irving*, p. 354
5. Ibid, p. 362
6. Terry, *Memoirs*, p. 174
7. Ibid, p. 154
8. Ibid
9. Ibid, p. 161
10. Irving, *Henry Irving*, p. 390
11. Sherrin, *Theatrical Anecdotes*, p. 127
12. Terry, *Memoirs*, p. 181

# *Notes*

13. Irving, *Henry Irving*, p. 467
14. Terry, *Memoirs*, p. 183
15. Irving, *Henry Irving*, p. 504
16. Auerbach, *Player in her Time*, p. 171

## CHAPTER NINE

1. Steen, *A Pride of Terrys*, p. 219
2. Terry, *Memoirs*, p. 236
3. Craig, *Ellen Terry and her Secret Self*, p. 121
4. Steen, *A Pride of Terrys*, p. 189
5. Irving, *Henry Irving*, p. 545
6. Sherrin, *Theatrical Anecdotes*, p. 128
7. Manvell, *Ellen Terry*, p. 251

## CHAPTER TEN

1. Manvell, *Ellen Terry*, p. 71
2. Craig, *Ellen Terry and her Secret Self*, p. 21
3. John Gielgud, private reminiscence to author, 1997
4. Ibid
5. Auerbach, *Player in her Time*, p. 295

# BIBLIOGRAPHY

Publishers' location is London.

Auerbach, Nina, *Player in her Time*, J.M. Dent and Sons Ltd, 1987

Craig, Edward Gordon, *Ellen Terry and her Secret Self*, Sampson Low, Marston and Co. Ltd, 1931

Gielgud, John, *Backward Glances*, Hodder and Stoughton, 1989

Irving, Laurence, *Henry Irving, the Actor and his World*, Faber and Faber, 1951

Manvell, Roger, *Ellen Terry*, Heinemann, 1968

St John, Christopher, *Ellen Terry*, Stars of the Stage series, John Lane, The Bodley Head, 1907

—— (ed.) *Ellen Terry and Bernard Shaw, A Correspondence*, Constable and Co. Ltd, 1931

Sherrin, Ned, *Ned Sherrin's Theatrical Anecdotes: a Connoisseur's Collection of Legends, Stories and Gossip*, Virgin Books, 1991

Steen, Marguerite, *A Pride of Terrys, Family Saga*, Longman, 1962

Terry, Ellen, *Ellen Terry's Memoirs*, with Preface, Notes and additional biographical chapters by Edith Craig and Christopher St John, Gollancz Ltd, 1933

# POCKET BIOGRAPHIES

## AVAILABLE

### *Beethoven*
Anne Pimlott Baker

### *Scott of the Antarctic*
Michael De-la-Noy

### *Alexander the Great*
E.E. Rice

### *Sigmund Freud*
Stephen Wilson

### *Marilyn Monroe*
Sheridan Morley and
Ruth Leon

### *Rasputin*
Harold Shukman

### *Jane Austen*
Helen Lefroy

### *Mao Zedong*
Delia Davin

*Ellen Terry*
Moira Shearer


*Abraham Lincoln*
H.G. Pitt


*Charles Dickens*
Catherine Peters


*David Livingstone*
C.S. Nicholls


## FORTHCOMING


*Marie and Pierre Curie*
John Senior


*Margot Fonteyn*
Alastair Macaulay


*Winston Churchill*
Robert Blake


*Enid Blyton*
George Greenfield

# FORTHCOMING

### *George IV*
Michael De-la-Noy

### *Christopher Wren*
James Chambers

### *W.G. Grace*
Donald Trelford

### *Che Guevara*
Andrew Sinclair

### *The Brontës*
Kathryn White

### *Martin Luther King*
Harry Harmer

### *Lawrence of Arabia*
Jeremy Wilson

### *Christopher Columbus*
Peter Riviere

For a copy of our complete list or details of other Sutton titles, please contact Regina Schinner at Sutton Publishing Limited, Phoenix Mill, Thrupp, Stroud, Gloucestershire, GL5 2BU

The Lee Strasberg Theatre & Film Institute
115 East 15th Street
New York, NY 10003
Tel: 212-533-5500